My Inspiring Journey (This Far)

*From the Enchanting Gambia to the
Intriguing Landscapes of Sweden*

By
Saul Jawara

MAPLE
PUBLISHERS

My Inspiring Journey (This Far): From the Enchanting Gambia to the Intriguing Landscapes of Sweden

Author: Saul Jawara

Copyright © Saul Jawara (2023)

The right of Saul Jawara to be identified as author of this work has been asserted by the author in accordance with section 77 and 78 of the Copyright, Designs and Patents Act 1988.

First Published in 2023

ISBN 978-1-83538-092-5 (Paperback)
      978-1-83538-037-6 (Hardback)
      978-1-83538-038-3 (E-Book)

Book Cover Design and Layout by:
    White Magic Studios
    www.whitemagicstudios.co.uk

Published by:
    Maple Publishers
    1 Brunel Way,
    Slough,
    SL1 1FQ, UK
    www.maplepublishers.com

Contents

Acknowledgements

Although my love for reading has been a lifelong passion, the thought of writing a book never crossed my mind until now. This marks my debut in the world of writing, and I couldn't be more elated to have brought this book to life.

The idea of writing a book has lingered in the backdrop of my life for quite some time. Among my dearest friends, especially a close friend who happens to be a doctor, the question of when I'd take the plunge into serious writing was a constant refrain. Their encouragement and unwavering support have been instrumental in my decision to finally embark on this journey.

Many of my friends and loved ones have enjoyed the stories and experiences I've shared over the years. It was their consistent inquiries about the arrival of this book that catalyzed my decision.

Moreover, I envisioned this book as a means to preserve and strengthen my connection with those who have played a profound role in shaping the person I've become. I want to express my deepest gratitude to my Mum, Dad, and Karin, even though they are no longer with us to witness this book's creation. Their influence continues to resonate within these pages.

I extend my heartfelt appreciation to Maple Publishers, my dedicated publisher, for their invaluable guidance and professionalism throughout the publishing process. Without their expertise, this endeavour wouldn't have been possible.

Chapter 1

My Childhood in The Gambia

I was born in Banjul, the capital of The Gambia, which happens to be the smallest mainland country in Africa. As an infant, my family relocated to Dakar, the neighbouring capital of Senegal, due to my Dad's contractual job. I resided in Dakar until the age of six when my uncle kindly brought me back to The Gambia to commence my education. Meanwhile, my parents remained in Dakar until a later time. Life in The Gambia was generally pleasant. Despite the substandard living conditions compared to the Western world, people enjoyed a moderate and decent quality of life. This small society fostered a strong sense of community, where individuals genuinely cared for one another. Despite having little, people found contentment and there was minimal social friction or tribal conflicts.

A spirit of mutual assistance prevailed, particularly towards the weaker and more vulnerable members of society. While it is true that a class system existed, it was rather ambiguous and did not create distinct divisions within society. In such a small population, we all lived and interacted with one another closely. We shopped at the same stores, visited the same markets, attended the same schools, traversed the same poorly maintained roads, and savoured similar types of food. During the 1960s and 1970s, the community consisted of only a few hundred thousand people. Sere Kunda, the city where I grew up and spent my childhood, thrived with vitality as the largest city in the country. The schools were sizable, accommodating possibly over a thousand students, equipped with well-constructed classrooms, expansive playgrounds, and competent teachers.

The school system's quality was much better there than elsewhere in the country, compared to the countryside. There were suitable professional teaching materials like textbooks, and the teachers, especially those I had, were well-trained. There were enough playing materials like balls, jumping ropes etc. School uniforms were an essential part of being at school; mine was always clean, ironed and well-fitted, sometimes coupled with sandals—looking smart was important. Special occasions like Independence Day, the 18th of February, always brought joyful moments that we all looked forward to as we marched to the capital Banjul in front of the President and other dignitaries. The preparations for that day each year were exciting as one gets new shoes, white socks and a new uniform! Going to the marching session was one of the most important events for every student in those days.

Thousands of students and teachers would usually take transport to Banjul where the march took place. The students would be put into files according to classes and age and then paraded in front of the head of state (the President) who would later give a speech to the thousands of students. We would then take transport back to our schools where everyone disperses. There was a free school feeding programme: nicely cooked cracked wheat for every child during the midday break. This was also an excellent initiative from the government, or wherever it was coming from in those days. Children learn and concentrate better when they are not hungry, and not all families can feed their children regularly. Those who did not like the food would prefer to bring their lunch or money to buy food, but there was help for those who could not afford to get food or purchase it from the school market. Going to school was fun with all the learning, games and food around!

The financial burden of school expenses weighed heavily on almost every family. Many families lived in relative poverty, and covering school expenses posed significant challenges, especially for those with large families. In those days, there was no concept of private schools, and children from the so-called middle and upper classes attended the same public schools. The absence of a government welfare system or assistance programme further compounded the struggle for families. Nevertheless, families persevered, and Mums, in particular, found innovative ways to sell goods and establish small businesses to afford school fees, funds, books, and even lunch money. Like my own experience, the majority of families relied heavily on their Mums' immense contributions to ensure their children's education. Regardless of a family's limited resources or financial means, the education of their children always remained a top priority.

Society thrived on a remarkable sense of solidarity, especially within extended families, neighbours, and friends. Uncles and aunties would occasionally step in to help with the financial burden of school expenses for children. Individualism was scarce in those times; instead, the focus was on sharing, assisting, and supporting one another. Although wages were meagre, many families managed to afford a bag of rice, which served as the country's staple food. Fish and vegetables were consistently affordable as well. The town centre housed a bustling daily market where traders and gardeners, particularly women from nearby villages, would gather to sell their produce. Throughout my childhood in The Gambia, I never witnessed cases of malnutrition. Hospitality was ingrained in our culture, and there was always an open invitation for anyone to share a meal. Moreover, there were often leftovers available for anyone to enjoy between meals.

During the 1960s and 1970s, it was a daily ritual for schools to provide milk to students before classes began. As an adult, I now understand the significance of this practice in boosting children's immune systems and keeping them healthy, particularly at a time when many families couldn't afford regular milk for their children. Consequently, everyone I encountered appeared well-nourished, disease-free, and in good health. While the health standards in The

Gambia may not have matched those of the Western world, access to healthcare was available and provided free of charge when needed, which greatly benefitted society. Almost every child received essential vaccinations such as the measles, mumps, and rubella (MMR) vaccine, as well as other immunizations after birth. Although there were areas for improvement, such as increasing the number of doctors, enhancing healthcare standards—especially in primary healthcare—and training community nurses, the healthcare system played a crucial role in maintaining the overall health of the population.

I cannot recall any significant disease outbreaks in the country during that time. While there were small public clinics and health centres spread across the country, the number of referral hospitals was limited. The Gambia thrived as a vibrant and harmonious blend of cultures, tribes, and religions, where everyone had their space and was respected regardless of their background. There were several cherished cultural activities, such as the 'Kankurang' dance event, where a person adorned their entire body with leaves and bark and danced to the beat of drums. Spectators would watch in awe and applaud the dancers. Another notable figure was the 'Kumpo', who concealed their entire body with tightly bound palm tree leaves, leaving only a long stick protruding from the top of their head. Drumming and dancing were popular cultural events performed by nearly every tribe in The Gambia, with women predominantly taking part in the dances while men portrayed the masked figures.

The Fulani tribe showcased their talent in combining songs and musical instruments with gymnastic-style dances, performed by strong and flexible men adorned in large, loose white trousers known as 'Chaya'. These trousers, made from several metres of fabric, would sway from side to side as the melodies played. The Gambian Creoles, also known as the Aku people, originally hailed from Sierra Leone and spoke Pidgin English. One of their cultural events featured a fully masked man dressed in elaborate, colourful garments, often wearing an animal-head figure, accompanied by drums and songs. The cultural season in The Gambia reached its peak after the summer season, typically from October through Christmas and into the New Year, extending until May when preparations for the upcoming summer farming season commenced. During this time, schools would close, the weather would become slightly cooler, drier, and favourable, and tourists would flock to the country. It was an ideal period for cultural activities to flourish.

The Christmas season, in particular, was a time of vibrant cultural celebrations. Despite over 90 per cent of the population being Muslim, the entire society enthusiastically embraced this Christian tradition. Schools closed, and families gathered to enjoy the festive atmosphere. The weather, usually a bit chilly, added to the ambience. Traditional activities included illuminated ship lanterns crafted from wooden frames and colourful patterned paper. A group of artists, including drummers and dancers, would lead the way, followed by a procession of hundreds of people, drumming, dancing, and collecting donations throughout the night. It was a time of unity and celebration, with people from all walks of life coming together. Just as with Islamic festivities, such as Eid, the population would joyfully gather and commemorate the occasion in perfect harmony. Love, tolerance, and acceptance were deeply embedded in the fabric of society, transcending ethnic groups, gender, and religious affiliations. Families, including mine, would celebrate together, sometimes attending church services alongside Christian neighbours and relatives, sharing meals and embracing the spirit of togetherness.

As I grew older, I discovered my passion for swimming. While most boys my age were engrossed in football, basketball, or athletics, I was always preoccupied with finding places to swim. Thankfully, in The Gambia, rivers and the sea were never too far from home. The country's boundaries, largely drawn by our former British colonial masters, closely followed the course of the long Gambia River, which starts from the Atlantic Ocean in the West and stretches eastward towards the easternmost part of Senegal. The Northern and Southern regions of the country are relatively narrow, often only a few kilometres wide from the riverbank to the Senegalese border. From my recollection, my Dad always had a job, either driving his taxi or working for a company. He would leave for work early in the morning, before anyone else in the family had even woken up, and return home in the evening.

When I was ten years old, I would occasionally take lunch to my Dad at his workplace during weekends. The taxi car park was just a short fifteen-minute walk from our home, and if he wasn't around, I would pass the lunch to someone else to give to him. On Sundays, when he didn't have to work, I would assist in cleaning the car. However, my relationship with my Dad wasn't as close as the bond I shared with my Mum. Our interactions were primarily based on commands and obedience. Although my Dad worked diligently, the income wasn't always sufficient. As a result, my Mum had to find ways to supplement the family's finances by selling various items or seeking employment opportunities. My Mum possessed a unique moral character, principles, and a serene demeanour that made her an extraordinary individual. She consistently endeavoured to instil in me and my siblings the values that would shape our lives with decency, respect, and a deep understanding of life's purpose.

We were fortunate to have all our basic needs met—ample food, clean clothes, and the means to attend school. My Mum took care of feeding us, offering guidance, and even injecting humour when needed, treating everyone with equality. I have vivid memories of the captivating stories she would share after dinner, stories that were both touching and grounded in reality. They remain alive within me to this day. My Mum embodied qualities of integrity, respect, and trust, exuding a serene majesty coupled with genuine humility. She effortlessly connected with people, making each feel important and valued. Despite being well-liked and known in the community, she had only one close friend who happened to be our neighbour just fifty metres away. My Mum had a natural maternal bond with me and provided the best advice that shaped my character, for which I am eternally grateful. As the eldest child, I was always by my Mum's side, acting as her right-hand helper and supporter.

I assisted her in raising my siblings, managing household chores, and even running errands, all while juggling my schooling. Despite my young age, I strived to alleviate any inconvenience or discomfort I noticed she experienced. I willingly offered my help and support without any complaints or hesitation, always obediently carrying out her instructions. This attitude of loyalty, respect, and dedication to my parents instilled in me a deep sense of empathy and sympathy towards others, including animals—a quality my Mum greatly appreciated. I was never a stubborn or headstrong child, and as a result, my Mum often praised me for the assistance and support I provided. Hearing her words of appreciation brought me immense contentment, joy, and a continued passion to serve the family. Perhaps this is why I developed a fondness for staying at home and staying busy within my immediate surroundings, always finding something worthwhile to engage in.

During those days, I found solace in helping my Mum immersing myself in personal projects such as gardening, taking care of poultry, or engaging in activities within the confines of my room like reading or rearranging furniture. This lifestyle played a significant role in shaping the individual I am today—someone who remains calm, content in solitude, and at ease with quietude. I was not the typical small boy who engaged in traditional boyhood activities that were commonly seen around. From an early age, I took responsibility for my clothes, washing and ironing them, and maintaining a sense of organization. As I grew older, these traits became more pronounced, and it was something that people in our community often talked about, as it was not customary for a young boy. However, my Mum always saw me as calm and unproblematic, and I am grateful to have possessed these qualities throughout my life. As time passed, I found myself increasingly interested in my surroundings and the world beyond.

I began to question many situations, particularly superstitious beliefs and cultural traditions. For instance, I resisted the common practice of eating with my hands, opting for a spoon, and drinking glass, with my water bottle instead. In Gambian society, a large portion of the population lacked formal education, leading to a deep acceptance of superstitious beliefs without questioning their validity. My challenges against these beliefs were driven by a desire to demonstrate their lack of logic, their unrealistic nature, and their inability to be proven. However, changing people's mindsets and altering their perception of deeply ingrained beliefs that had been passed down for generations proved to be a formidable task. In response to my questioning and resistance, I was often labelled as 'Toubab', which means 'Whiteman' in the local language. It was a term used to denote someone who challenged traditional beliefs and customs. Interestingly, after living in Europe for several decades, I realized that even Europeans held onto superstitious beliefs, especially among the older generation. This realization highlighted that superstitions transcend cultural boundaries and can be found in various societies.

My behaviour and attitude towards these beliefs were to try to prove everything, how things work, why things happen, and practise simple common sense, and that became more ingrained into me as I grew up. I asked more questions and refused to believe things blindly, instead used reasoning to solve problems and find out *why* things are the way they are. In a society where children are not allowed to ask questions or have an opinion, I became an outsider, designated as rude, too Western and thought I know it all. During the days when the other three boys and I went through the ritual of circumcision(which every boy has to go through to become a man), we lived in a small isolated house. The older boys wanted to instil fear into us by telling us that a mysterious devil would be coming for a visit. As is widely believed traditionally, this spirit is aggressive and dangerous, so we the newly circumcised must behave, be disciplined and not try to even look up or have any eye contact with him despite whatever noise we heard around the house, and if one paid real attention to what these guys were saying with seriousness, everything was fearful, especially to children.

The lights were turned off after a while, the silence, the darkness inflicting more fear on us; suddenly there was a strange noise that was difficult to distinguish. So, we all lay down and hid our faces as much as possible so as not to have any eye contact with the devil that might come into the house. After a very short while, the noise outside stopped, and the lights were on again. Everyone was staring at each other and even scared to utter a word. The older boys also acted fearfully that danger had arrived and was still outside the house, just scaring us more. We later discovered that this kind of game was part of the circumcision tradition, including singing traditional songs and stories. Suddenly, from outside came a person who looked like he knew nothing about the noise, then he sat down breathing heavily after the running he did around the house, but trying to cover up the heavy breathing.

As I observed his expression, it became evident that he was hiding something he didn't want us to know. At that moment, I boldly stated, "I know he was the one making that noise outside, running around the house trying to scare us. There was no actual devil, just him outside making all that noise." The older boys exchanged glances and burst into laughter, intrigued by how I had uncovered their scheme. They asked me how I had figured it out, and I replied, "I don't believe in the devil you were trying to scare us with." Curiosity was piqued, and one of the boys proceeded to demonstrate how they created the noise by tying a string to the end of a hacksaw blade and swinging it around at high speed, producing the eerie sound. I revealed their scare tactics, which were meant to intimidate and control our fear. They would use the threat of calling the devil to make us behave or do what they wanted. It reminded me of how in the West, they would create the idea of Santa Claus as something real but imaginary, using it as a means to reward or punish children based on their behaviour. "Behave, be obedient, or conform, otherwise Santa will not bring you a present," they would say.

Reflecting on the experience, I recognized that the entire circumcision episode was a result of cultural, traditional, and religious practices aimed at preparing us to become mature men and responsible individuals in society. However, there were instances where superstitions intertwined with these practices. I recalled an uncle who once visited us and claimed to possess a juju, a superstitious charm believed to bestow magical powers. He asserted that no knife could penetrate his skin as long as he had the juju on him. I strongly disputed this claim, finding it impossible to comprehend. Nevertheless, in the Gambia, many people believed that the village called Balangarra, where he hailed from, possessed expertise in creating such jujus. I struggled to make sense of the idea that having a juju on your body could grant someone magical powers that would prevent any knife from penetrating your skin. How could that be possible?

At that moment, I was determined to challenge my uncle and demand proof of his juju's effectiveness. However, I was not willing to hand over the knife to him to demonstrate it on my skin. Instead, I proposed an alternative idea. I suggested using a cock from my poultry flock and tying the juju to the bird, then attempting to slaughter it as a test of the juju's power. Surprisingly, my uncle accepted the challenge and confidently asserted that the knife would not be able to penetrate the bird, despite my strong disagreement. I called upon my younger brother to fetch a fowl from the flock, and once the bird was in our possession, we proceeded to tie the juju onto its wing. We were prepared to put the juju to the test and determine its efficacy. My uncle instructed me to carry out the slaughter, and reluctantly, I complied.

As I brought the knife down upon the fowl, blood splattered everywhere—on the knife, my hands, and the ground. At that moment, I jumped back, abandoning the fowl and tossing the knife aside. Five onlookers had gathered, anticipating a miracle or some manifestation of magical powers. However, the outcome was far from miraculous. It was clear to me and everyone present that the juju had no protective power against the knife—it was all a hoax. Laughter erupted among the spectators, and I confidently declared, "Look, I told you there is no protective juju against a knife. It's all a hoax!" The laughter continued as my uncle stood there, disappointed, ashamed, and disgraced. The lifeless fowl lay on the ground as a stark reminder of the failed demonstration. I washed my hands, handed my uncle the useless juju, and firmly told him, "You cannot continue to wear this. You have witnessed firsthand that it does not work. What do you need it for? It's not working!" More laughter ensued from the friends who had witnessed the unfolding episode between my uncle and me. The slaughtered fowl was made dinner that evening.

I was once taken by surprise when the Member of Parliament representing the ruling party in our constituency approached my Mum and asked her to lead a women's group. Despite my Mum's reputation as a non-political person, she accepted the responsibility, fully aware of the significance of the role. The women's group, affiliated with the People's Progressive Party (PPP), decided to hold their monthly meetings at our residence. These gatherings disrupted the tranquillity and peacefulness that I cherished, as approximately 50 women would gather at our house for the meetings. The group was well-structured, with a secretary, a treasurer, and my Mum as the leader. They engaged in various activities, fundraised, and managed their affairs with great diligence.

To create some personal space during their meetings, I would often retreat to the beach until their session concluded in the evening, typically around seven o'clock. I can recall a few instances when they organized traditional drumming and dancing events, although those activities did not captivate my interest during my childhood. Traditional drumming had never been a source of entertainment for me. The women's group continued to thrive until my Mum fell ill. In our relatively small family of six, consisting of two girls and three boys, we grew up together, except for one younger brother who lived with an uncle in Kaur to attend school in the countryside. Kaur was also the place where we underwent circumcision. After completing his education, he returned and reunited with the rest of the family.

The only thing that deviated from the norm in our family was one of my younger brothers' tendencies to cry excessively without any apparent reason. My Mum tried everything within her power to alleviate his crying behaviour, but her efforts proved futile. People would often suggest to my Mum that she should consult a doctor to investigate whether he had an underlying medical condition or pain. My Mum visited several doctors in search of answers as to why my brother would cry incessantly. However, the doctors couldn't find any issues with him and predicted that he would eventually outgrow this behaviour as he grew older. Mum and I would sometimes take turns attempting everything imaginable to soothe him. Nights were particularly challenging for everyone; he would exert extra effort and display more energy than ever, sometimes crying until the early morning hours before finally becoming tired and falling asleep. I would seize the opportunity to rest for a few hours before getting up and preparing for school. This ongoing situation somehow had an impact on my schooling, and I always arrived in class tired and sleepy.

We didn't always have household maids, but during the times we did, they would alleviate the burdensome tasks of assisting my Mum and trying to calm my little crying brother. The maids would be occupied with laundry and ensuring the cleanliness of the premises. They would leave around seven in the evening and return to work by eight in the morning. However, I took on the responsibility of caring for my clothes—washing, ironing, and sewing them when necessary. When I reached around 15 years old, I had my little room located at the corner of the main house, providing me with privacy. I had a radio and a bicycle that served me well, especially for commuting to school or visiting the beach. Today, as an adult, I harbour no regrets and feel immensely grateful that my childhood experiences taught me responsibility and instilled in me discipline and organizational skills. I attribute these qualities to my upbringing.

I have absorbed a wealth of wisdom from my Mum through listening to her and obeying her teachings. She instilled in me values such as abstaining from smoking or drinking, showing respect to everyone, and embodying humility and kindness towards all individuals, regardless of familiarity. These guiding principles, repeatedly emphasized by my Mum, still resonate within me. Growing up, I took on responsibilities typically associated with girls e.g. domestic work, such as caring for my siblings, cooking, and engaging in various household tasks. This closeness with my Mum fostered a deep empathy for women in general and their ongoing struggles for gender equity, equal pay, leadership opportunities, empowerment, and combating domestic violence, among other important issues. Later, my genuine passion for swimming consumed me, often leading me to prioritize it over any other activity. I would venture to the nearby beach, a few kilometres away in Banjul, or to the river situated just a kilometre behind our house, flowing towards Banjul.

It was all about swimming and conquering challenges, whether it be navigating strong currents or swimming longer distances. Alongside swimming, I also developed an interest in fishing. There were numerous occasions when Mum became angry, urging me to refrain from going to the sea due to its inherent dangers, especially when there were reports in the media about people drowning. Naturally, she felt fearful, uneasy, and concerned about my frequent swimming escapades. However, nothing could deter me from my beloved activity, particularly on Saturdays—I simply couldn't resist its allure! There was one day in Banjul when I swam too far out. The tide was receding, and the current was exceptionally strong. As I turned back towards the pier, I noticed how minuscule people appeared standing there, and a sense of worry crept into my mind. I began to question whether I would be able to make it back, especially while swimming against the prevailing current. In that poignant moment, I contemplated the possibility of drowning and the impact it would have on my Mum's life if I were to meet such a tragic fate.

In a matter of seconds, as various thoughts raced through my mind, I made a resolute decision: I was not going to succumb to fate. Instead, I chose to succeed in swimming back, no matter the challenges that lay ahead. Employing the front-crawl stroke, which proved more effective against the strong current from the opposing side, I propelled myself towards the distant harbour where onlookers stood watching. At times, it felt as though I was making no progress, but I refused to let fatigue overtake me and pressed on, unwavering in my determination. Despite the arduousness of the journey and the considerable distance that separated me from my destination, I finally reached the wooden pier. Upon reaching the pier, I realized the extent of my exhaustion when I attempted to grip the iron ladder that extended from the top of the wooden platform and hung down into the water. Though I managed to hold onto the ladder, I lacked the strength to hoist myself up onto the wooden platform. So, with my body still immersed in the water, I released the air from my lungs and mouth in a manner reminiscent of someone completing a marathon.

I continued to catch my breath heavily while clinging to the ladder, allowing myself around ten minutes to recover. Eventually, I mustered the energy to climb the ladder slowly, until I could finally collapse onto the wooden surface, where I remained for quite some time. I distinctly recall hearing someone comment that they thought I would never make it. After gathering my wits, I changed into dry clothes, packed my belongings, and set out to find a taxi to take me home. That perilous experience served as a wake-up call, reminding me of the need for caution when venturing too far out to sea. This incident could have easily claimed my life. We frequently heard news reports of drowning incidents broadcasted over the radio, further reinforcing the inherent dangers. At home, we had a medium-sized Phillips transistor that remained mostly on throughout the daytime, relaying news, updates and music.

During the 1970s, the music scene was vibrant with iconic artists such as Elton John, Stevie Wonder, Marvin Gaye, James Brown, Abba, John Lennon, Bob Marley, Earth, Wind and Fire, The O'Jays, Elvis Presley, Temptations, Commodores, Barry White, and Mo-Town artists, all reaching the pinnacle of their careers. One of the most popular and modern radio stations during that time was Radio Syd, which came from Skane, Sweden, settled in the Gambia and was owned by a

Swedish guy called Conny. Since 1968, with the influx of Scandinavian tourists, the station also broadcasted news in the Swedish language every morning and evening. Music played a significant role in our household, with ample time dedicated to listening to the artists and songs of that time. Additionally, our home featured a small vinyl record player with a couple of albums, including works by Elvis Presley and Santana. Mum held a great fondness for Elvis's music. Owning my first camera was a source of immense pride for me, which happened in the early 1970s when I was around twelve years old. It was a Kodak 110, and I cherished it dearly, recognizing that not everyone possessed such a device that many dreamed of having.

I proudly showcased my camera, wanting everyone to be aware of my ownership. Another significant aspect of my childhood was movies. I had the opportunity to watch American Hollywood and Indian movies, as Indian production companies dominated the movie market in The Gambia at that time. As mentioned earlier, at the age of six, when it was time for me to begin school, my Dad's elder brother (who shares my name) travelled to Senegal, where my Dad was working and living, to collect me and bring me back to The Gambia. I brought along a multitude of toys eg cars, trucks, marbles, and more. My uncle was a serene and solitary individual, often referred to by the nickname "The King" due to his calm and softspoken demeanour.

During the weekends, my uncle's wife, whom I affectionately called Mum, would receive movie money from him, and we would regularly visit the cinema on Fridays and Saturdays. She took exceptional care of me when my parents were away working in Dakar, Senegal. During our regular weekend movie-going, I once experienced post-traumatic stress disorder (PTSD) after watching a horror movie. Even with an adult by my side, I struggled to sleep for days, haunted by the graphic scenes that played in my mind whenever I closed my eyes. Eventually, they took me to the hospital, where I stayed for a few days. In those days, there were no age restrictions for horror movies. Alongside the horror films, we enjoyed a wide range of Western cowboy movies, Roman gladiator movies, and the latest releases from Bollywood every Monday. The major actors were well-known, and some locals even attempted to speak a bit of Hindi and embrace elements of Indian culture. I was frightened by Arab movies that often featured intense sword-fighting and killing scenes.

Aside from our cinema outings as a small boy, my daily routine revolved around attending school, returning home to water the flowers and plants—including mango, guava, pawpaw, and banana plants—and playing with my toys. After a couple of years, my parents returned to The Gambia and joined us, as my Dad's contract with the Senegalese company had come to an end. It was a joyous reunion for me. Dad bought a dark blue Ford Cortina taxi, and we all resided at my uncle's place near the main road. We continued our tradition of weekend movies, with my Mum joining us. Outside the cinema premises, there were always vendors selling various items like roasted peanuts, fruits, candy mints, and chewing gums. We lived harmoniously and peacefully for a few years until the arrival of my younger sister, prompting my Dad to seek a more spacious living arrangement.

My first cousin, my uncle's first child, an older girl in those days perhaps in her 20s, tall, agile and stubborn, also lived with us. Everyone had difficulty getting along with her, especially her parents. She was a huge bully; she would swear, use foul words disrespectfully, never go to school and smoke cigarettes, something projected as bad behaviour in that society, especially for a young girl. My Mum, who arrived a couple of months earlier from Senegal, had repeatedly tried to avoid any confrontation with her. She was the most disreputable family member who started going out to nightclubs, smoking and drinking in her early teens. As she was too young to go out at night, she waited until everyone was asleep, and then she would slowly go through the back window and come back early in the morning. Every type of disciplinary action had been tried on her to change her behaviour.

As a child, I was profoundly afraid of her; I would not look her straight in the eyes. She would send me places to buy her cigarettes or beer, which I would wrap in a towel so people could not see, but I always obeyed her. She would yell at me and give me instructions to do things for her and continued bullying me. I was too little and scared of her. Mum didn't like what was going on but also tried to avoid offending her or encountering any confrontation with her. Mum rather kept quiet and always ignored her. Hence, she never laid her hands on me or hit me physically. However, one Saturday afternoon, around midday, I had a couple of mangoes with me; she got mad and insisted that I must give the mangoes to her. These were from mango trees that I had attended to and looked after daily, watering them for years. My Mum was cooking lunch and pounding spices using the pestle and mortar made out of wood.

Mum told her to leave me alone and stop the bullying and intimidation; she did not own the mangoes that I had looked after for years. Her Dad, my uncle, had then gone to the countryside on a trip transporting peanuts, and her Mum, who had a restaurant, was not at home yet. Suddenly, she decided to attack my Mum physically. My Mum used the pestle, hitting her on the forehead. Instantaneously, she fell to the ground, fainted, bleeding heavily on the forehead, kicking and screaming. My Mum went out to the main road, got a taxi, and they rushed to the Royal Victoria Hospital in Banjul, which is about 15 minutes from home. Her head had a large bandage on it when she came back home a couple of hours later. When her Mum returned home in the evening, she was angry with her and attempted to punish her even further for trying to fight my Mum; hence my Mum intervened. Forty years after this incident, she still carries the scar mark on the left side of her forehead the last time I saw her.

This incident was how I also obtained my freedom from her until we moved elsewhere, but not too far from their place. As I became a bit older at the age of 16, I was mentally mature and knew what to get involved in or not, what I wanted in life and how I wanted to live my future. I already had chosen my life pattern. The famous Radio

Station, Radio Syd played a significant part in my early life. It was the primary source of knowing what was going on in current worldwide affairs, and mostly where I could listen to BBC programmes. There have been many times when I cycled on the beach and passed tourists lying naked, or cycling in town with very little covering their bodies. Many local boys on the beach followed and tried to make friends with these tourists, which was how many boys and men fell in love or forged friendship with many Scandinavians.

Indeed, during that time in the Gambia, many individuals found themselves being taken to Scandinavia through their associations with older or younger foreign women. Tourism played a significant role in the country's economy, benefitting various sectors such as taxi drivers, traders, souvenir stores, hotels, and subcontractors. It was a time when pen friendships were popular among students. Engaging in correspondence with pen pals through letters and exchanging pictures was a common practice, and I benefitted greatly from it too. Some Gambians even had the opportunity to meet their pen pals in person and develop relationships, eventually leading to the chance to move to Scandinavia. While I never personally engaged in deep conversations with tourists, I would often cycle past them without interacting extensively.

The preference for solitude and independent thinking was something that came naturally to me; it was a behaviour I embraced without being explicitly taught. I enjoyed being alone, thinking for myself, and carrying out tasks independently, which led people to describe me as a reserved individual. When others commented to my Mum about my reticence, she would simply respond, "Oh yeah, he's always been like that." Although I don't recall fights or disagreements with others as a child. I would often express my desire to travel extensively around the world when I grew up. These comments would sometimes elicit laughter from those around me. I always had a sense that I wanted to venture beyond the borders of the Gambia as I got older. In those times, travel was relatively straightforward for

Africans—obtain a passport, purchase a ticket, and set off on your journey, no visas or invitation letters required.

Maintaining good hygiene has always been a priority for me since childhood. It was customary for people to wash their hands before eating with their hands, but I preferred to use my spoon and my water dispenser which I never allowed others to use. I valued cleanliness and took precautions to ensure good hygiene to the fullest. There was a tradition of brewing green tea, known as Ataya, where people would sit around and wait for each person to be served a half-filled glass. I found this practice unpleasant and time-consuming. I also considered it unhygienic since everyone would drink from the same glass without rinsing it, which could potentially transmit diseases. So, I was never interested in drinking Ataya or I would be served in my glass or cup.

Education has played a significant role in my life since early on, and it continues to be essential to me today. I have always had a strong thirst for knowledge and would constantly read anything I could get my hands on. Although I started reading novels at a young age, I often had limited time to fully concentrate on them due to domestic responsibilities, helping Mum, and other interests I pursued. During those times, teachers were highly qualified, mostly having completed teachers' college as qualified teachers. Their expertise and dedication were reflected in their teaching methods and practices. I have always been fascinated by language and enjoyed writing. However, one of the challenges to education during that period was the cost of finances and other expenses associated with schooling, especially expensive textbooks among other things.

As a young person, I demonstrated a high level of organization, whether it was in maintaining my room, taking care of my clothes, cooking nutritious meals, or engaging in cyling or swimming. I exhibited maturity and discipline beyond my years, which led me to develop friendships with older and more successful individuals. These qualities and experiences have become ingrained in my personality and have shaped who I am today.

The Gambian society was characterized by openness, harmony, and a strong sense of community. People knew and supported one another, whether they were neighbours, friends, relatives or even the unknown. My Dad was often occupied with work, sometimes even on weekends. I became attuned to the sound of his car engine, and I could easily recognize it when he arrived home. I sparked my fascination with cars and developed an immense interest in them. I would even guess the make and model of cars simply by listening to the sound of their engines. Occasionally, I had the opportunity to sit beside my Dad as he drove, observing his actions closely. I believed that driving a car was something I could easily do myself. One of my favourite tasks was washing the car including the engine on weekends. Gradually, I started venturing out on my own without my Dad's authorization or acknowledgement.

As I grew older, my interest in cars deepened, and I became adept at identifying different car brands, models, their countries of origin and the mechanical aspects of cars. During the evenings, whenever time allowed, I would take my bicycle and ride to the beach, covering a distance of approximately ten kilometres. Sometimes, I would time my ride to coincide with the sunset, reaching the beach just as the sun dipped below the horizon of the Atlantic Ocean. It was a breathtaking sight that I cherished. Along the beach, particularly during low tide, I would cycle for about five kilometres, passing by landmarks such as the BB Hotel and Fajara Hotel, before making my way back home through Pipeline Road. Later, I started spending time at one of the most prominent auto repair workshops in town. I would hang around, observing the mechanics as they repaired engines and gained a better understanding of vehicles. The workshop serviced various types of vehicles, including tractors, graders, huge trucks and cars of all kinds, providing me with a diverse range of knowledge in engine mechanics.

The children belonging to the owner of the vehicle workshop became my companions, and we had a marvellous time together, frequently venturing in and out of the open garage, getting ourselves dirty, and occasionally lending a hand to the mechanics. The most thrilling moments occurred during the summer break from school. The owner of the workshop, who possessed a fleet of vehicles, including tractors, would entrust three of us teenagers with a tractor to venture into the countryside for periods lasting two to three days. Our task was to plough fields for private farmers. At the end of our journey, we would return home with a bag full of cash, then he would give us a token of appreciation, a modest sum for each of us. However, our joy stemmed not from the money itself, but from the adventure and amusement we experienced, driving, ploughing, and independently fixing any breakdowns the tractor encountered. Fortunately, my Mum was generous enough to allow me to embark on these escapades, which granted me extensive knowledge about vehicles and the ability to drive at a remarkably young age. I bear the scars from those times, a constant reminder of the expertise I gained that will never fade away.

There was a night when an unfortunate accident occurred. I was swiftly transported to Victoria, the main hospital, by a taxi from the rural area to the capital city of Banjul, approximately 30 kilometres away from where the incident took place. It was well past midnight, and as I drove with one hand, the other rested on the frame of the plough at the back. Unknowingly, I pressed the lever that lowered the weighty plough into the ground. As the colossal iron frame descended, I failed to realize that my thumb was positioned beneath the main iron bar, right where the heavy plough was meant to rest. It came crashing down on my thumb, crushing a portion of it. A cry of pain escaped my lips, and I promptly turned off the engine. One of my friends rushed over and lifted the plough from my injured thumb. Blood gushed forth, and the tip of my thumb was flattened by the force of the impact. The following morning, on a Saturday, I returned home with a prominent white bandage adorning my hand.

My Mum was devastated when she saw me, but I reassured her that it was just a minor cut that needed to be bandaged to prevent infection. Thankfully, the wound healed after a couple of weeks. I was relieved that it didn't happen during the school period, sparing me any additional complications.

At the age of 15, I began joining my friends for weekly hunting excursions sometimes, primarily on Saturdays. We would venture into the wilderness for about three to five hours, chatting and having fun, usually returning with a catch, often a rabbit or more. There came a time when I caught two small rabbits and decided to keep them as pets. I constructed a beautiful cage, spacious enough, using wood and wire, and provided them with plenty of lettuce and carrots. During this period, I also had four small white rats freely roaming around the house. Little did I know that having this combination of animals in such proximity was a recipe for disaster. I learned this lesson the hard way.

One morning, I woke up to a heartbreaking sight. My two rabbits had been devoured by the white rats. They had managed to breach the cage, killing the rabbits and feasting on the soft parts of their faces— particularly their lips and noses. I felt a mixture of disappointment and anger, as I had intended to raise and care for those rabbits. It was a significant setback for me.

On a beautiful Saturday, following a hunting expedition with friends, my Mum called me aside and asked, "How was your experience catching that rabbit today?" I replied, "It was quite challenging. We had to chase it for kilometres before finally capturing it!" She then imparted some wisdom, saying, "You know, that rabbit didn't want to die. It was running for its life. I think you should consider stopping the hunting of these animals." Her words struck a chord within me, and I began to feel a deep sense of remorse. I reflected on how these animals fought tirelessly to survive, attempting to escape from the clutches of the two ferocious Old English Sheepdogs owned by our neighbours.

These dogs formed a close bond with me and always displayed great enthusiasm for our Saturday hunting outings. However, that marked the end of my hunting career. I never explicitly mentioned what my Mum had said to my friends, but I insisted that I had decided to stop hunting, and the saddest part for them was that if I didn't participate in the hunting the dogs wouldn't follow them. Consequently, everyone else ceased their hunting activities. One day, my Mum gave me money to go to the central market, which was approximately a 20-minute walk from home, to purchase meat—specifically, cow meat (beef) according to our Muslim dietary practices. I made my way to the market and headed straight to the section where the butchers were stationed. The first meat I laid my eyes upon was in a large pile, fresh and reasonably priced as I discovered upon inquiring. I believed it was an excellent deal, considering the amount of money I had in my possession. Satisfied with my purchase, I couldn't help but sing some of the best songs I could recall as I walked home, carrying the bag of fresh meat. When I arrived home, I excitedly explained to my Mum what a fantastic bargain I had secured—the meat was abundant and affordable. I fetched a large bowl and placed the meat inside.

However, as my Mum laid her eyes on it, she lowered her head and asked, "What is this?" She continued, "It's pork!" I stood there, dumbfounded and taken aback by the surprise revelation. Disappointment washed over me, leaving me motionless and filled with regret. "Take the meat back and get a refund!" she exclaimed. I dutifully returned to the butcher, who accepted the meat and refunded my money. Later, my Mum took the time to explain the differences between pork and beef to me. This incident soon became a humorous anecdote, and everyone began laughing and teasing me for days. My supposedly great deal had turned into a comical and laughable story. Since that day, Mum never entrusted me with the task of buying meat again, and it remained a lighthearted memory within our family.

The Gambia, both in the past and present, has been considered underdeveloped by international standards. However, despite this, every family was able to afford three square meals. As previously mentioned, our medical and health system was quite impressive, even earning recognition from an American friend who was a doctor and had worked in other African countries and conducted studies for the CDC. According to him, our healthcare system was one of the best in Africa. However, when I had the opportunity to travel to Senegal, our closest neighbouring country, I realized the stark contrast in terms of development. Witnessing the advancements and progress in Senegal made me realize that our government in The Gambia had not been successful in driving the country's development, even decades after gaining independence, despite all the rhetoric.

That being said, I continued to appreciate and enjoy what our country had to offer: peace, tranquillity, solitude (which I cherished immensely), and a sense of comfort. With a population in the hundreds of thousands, there were no traffic congestions or crowded marketplaces; life was simple. It was a laid-back and relaxed lifestyle in the country. Soon after Gambian independence, we started receiving visitors as tourists from Sweden, Denmark, and Norway. My generation grew up exposed to Scandinavian tourists, familiar with their languages, music, movies, and magazines, which provided glimpses of the outside world. In those days, the summer holiday period was highly anticipated by everyone. It was a time when families, friends, and loved ones had the opportunity to visit for an extended period, have fun, and deepen their connections. The summer season held a distinct and special charm, unlike any other time of the year, and it commenced in June.

During August, heavy rain was a common occurrence, sometimes persisting for days during the holiday season. The landscape transformed into vibrant greenery as grass and trees flourished. Insects, once absent, would re-emerge, buzzing with life and creating a symphony of sounds in the summer air. For me, summer and holidays meant embarking on a journey to visit my grandparents in the countryside—a day-long expedition in those times. The roads, composed of uneven red stones and riddled with potholes, presented a challenging path. Along the way, we would encounter a ferry crossing on the River Gambia, where we would spend hours patiently waiting for the ferry to transport us from the south bank to the north bank and vice versa. As a child, undertaking a tiring yet thrilling day of travel spanning a mere 180 kilometres was no easy feat. I felt a mix of anticipation and anxiety, but my enthusiasm for the trip never waned.

My granddad's farm boasted plenty of cows and three horses, which served as my primary source of motivation for the journey. The presence of abundant fresh milk and the opportunity to meet many relatives from Mum's side, whom I had either not known or only heard about, added to the excitement. They would take me on tours of the compound and the neighbouring areas to greet people. This small Gambian village, secluded and lacking electricity or conspicuous signs of modern living, exuded a sense of freedom, happiness, and peace in its unique way. The residents would occasionally travel to the town when they needed supplies, only to return to the serenity of the village. I recall some of my uncles and aunties visiting for a few weeks, sometimes bringing gifts like roasted rice and milk. As a shy and cautious child, I yearned for adventure. The prospect of visiting the horses in the barn thrilled me no end—they allowed me to touch them and gaze into their eyes, a bit intimidating due to their sheer size.

However, I quickly realized that the horses were friendly creatures and posed no harm to anyone. They were robust, healthy, and imposing, making me appear tiny in comparison. Most of the time, they exhibited a calm and majestic demeanour. The disparities between the urban area and the countryside were evident in attitudes, lifestyles, and even language. People would remark that my spoken language was not pure, highlighting the cultural differences that made me feel like a visitor and an outsider. As a result, the local children referred to me as 'toubab', a term meaning white man. Since I was a guest, I had to accept such terms and names, even if I chose to ignore them. Another thrilling moment occurred in the evening when the cows returned home. Participating in activities like tying them up and milking them filled me with excitement. Learning the technique and process of milking cows took some time, and my limited visits to the countryside did not provide sufficient opportunities to acquire skills like horseback riding.

On one occasion, we ventured to my granddad's groundnut farm, a few kilometres away from the village, where we spent the entire day. As the sun began to set, signalling the time to head home, one of my uncles had the idea of placing me on a horse so I could ride back as they walked alongside me. As we started our journey home, the horse suddenly began to trot, gradually distancing itself from the rest of the group. Fear gripped me as I had ridden a horse before, and panic set in as the trotting grew faster, leaving the others far behind. I desperately attempted to halt the horse, but lacking knowledge of the proper commands or techniques, I struggled to do so. The pace of the trotting intensified, and I found it challenging to maintain my balance. I swayed from side to side, struggling to hold on in the middle. Behind me, was my uncle and others shouting, urging me to grip the horse's mane tightly, which I did while continuing my efforts to slow down— or at least control—the horse's speed.

Soon, I realized that the horse was galloping, its powerful strides carrying us forward at an incredible speed. "Hold on tight!" my uncle's voice echoed from behind once again. I clung onto the horse's mane with all my strength as my shirt flapped wildly behind me like a kite in the wind. We raced through the bushes and onto the sandy path road, the horse's speed only increasing as we approached the village and our home. Fear consumed me, and I felt utterly helpless, relying solely on the horse's movements. In a matter of minutes, we arrived in the village, the horse showing no signs of slowing down as we passed a large crowd of people gathered under the shade of a majestic tree at the village centre. "Oh, it's the Tubab," they all noticed and pointed out. The horse continued straight to our home, gradually reducing its speed as we neared. Finally, it came to a stop, and I quickly dismounted before it retreated into the safety of the barn. I stood there in a state of shock, my emotions in turmoil.

Though shaken and trembling, I couldn't help but feel a sense of pride that I had successfully ridden this colossal horse from the farm without falling or injuring myself. Gradually, my heart rate slowed, and a unique sense of accomplishment washed over me—I had made it, Wow! Eventually, my uncle and the others arrived home, and the incident became the talk of the evening. However, rather than sparking an interest in horse riding, the experience deepened my fear of riding. I refused my uncle's repeated encouragement to learn, convinced that the horse would once again run out of control. From that day forward, I never attempted to ride horses again. Leaving the countryside after spending weeks there was always a bittersweet moment. The food was different and delightful, and the people were kind-hearted and welcoming.

During one summer school break, I had the opportunity to visit a town not too far from my grandparents' place. This town was bustling with large markets, enormous stores, a central cinema, hospitals, and other modern landmarks. What I thought would be a typical holiday turned out to be a unique experience - my circumcision. During this time, I stayed at my Dad's side uncle's house. He was well-known for being a skilled tailor, specializing in sewing school uniforms. One morning, after three days of staying at his place, he took me, my younger brother and another uncle's son to the hospital, then I learned that we were going for a circumcision. Although I felt scared and nervous, I managed to maintain my composure. Upon arriving at the hospital, we entered a spacious waiting room and inquired about the doctor. It appeared to be a weekend as there were only a few people around.

Suddenly, a well-groomed, middle-aged man emerged, and I recognized him as the doctor. After exchanging greetings with my uncle, the doctor kindly greeted us and assured us that the process would be painless. His words helped to ease my nerves and instil confidence in me. It was evident that the time had come for the procedure. I was provided with a green patient gown and guided to a raised operating bed. I lay down on my back while a green surgical cloth with a hole was draped over my front, and the doctor began the operation. I experienced a slight sting during the initial two anaesthetic injections, but after that, I felt nothing. Approximately 15 to 20 minutes later, the doctor removed the cloth and exclaimed, "It's finished now!"

Circumcision had always been associated with pain and a lengthy healing process in my mind. As per our religious tradition, it was something every male had to undergo. However, I had no idea that the entire procedure would be so quick and painless. I got off the operating bed, waiting for my younger brother and another cousin to undergo the same procedure. Afterwards, we were taken home, just a few minutes away from the hospital. We received excellent care, and within about three weeks, we had fully healed and emerged as real men. I returned home weeks after everything had concluded. One day, we had an unexpected visitor. A man arrived unannounced, claiming to be from our village and a relative with the same surname as my Dad, Jawara.

My Mum believed him and warmly welcomed him, providing him with a well-organised guest room. He didn't mention the duration of his stay or the purpose of his visit. In the evening, Mum assumed that he might not have eaten anything during his journey, so she served him a generous medium-sized bowl of meat stew with rice and vegetables. Then around nine or ten years old, I took the bowl of food to his room after knocking on the door. I placed the food down and informed him that it was his dinner. He thanked me, and I left the room. Saturday morning arrived, and by nine o'clock, we had not heard from him or seen him. Concerned, Mum decided to check if he was awake or still asleep. The sun was already up, casting its hot rays, and there was complete silence from the guest room. To our surprise, we discovered that the room was empty; he had already packed his belongings and left earlier.

Mum and I approached the door, which was slightly open. She knocked, but there was no response. Slowly, she pushed the door open, revealing an empty room with only the empty dinner bowl from the previous night sitting in the centre. We stepped inside, but Mum came out and proceeded to the back of the house to ensure everything was alright. Suddenly, she called me over to witness something she had discovered. To my dismay, I found faeces scattered all over the floor, with flies already feasting on the unpleasant sight. It was a repulsive and foul-smelling scene. I couldn't help but exclaim, "How could he do such a thing?" Mum calmly suggested, "Well, perhaps he had over-eaten and felt embarrassed to ask for the toilet." We reluctantly proceeded to clean up the area.

As part of my daily routine for many years, Mum would give me a tablespoon of cod liver oil and another spoonful of a locally made dark and extremely bitter liquid called 'Tulukuna.' This was a morning ritual before heading to school every day. The school was only a ten-minute walk away, but on the way back in the afternoons, I would sometimes throw stones to knock down ripe mangoes hanging from the branches of trees. These mango trees belonged to someone or were situated within someone's compound, with their branches extending outside onto the streets, making them accessible to people passing by. I targeted these trees and occasionally managed to bring some mangoes home, even though we didn't have our mango tree at that time. Playing with the neighbourhood kids who were of the same age group provided me with the opportunity to enjoy football games and free mangoes, which I would occasionally bring back with me.

My Mum had an uncle who served as a head teacher in a primary school located in the countryside. He would frequently visit our home on weekends, always appearing calm and composed. I never heard him raise his voice, regardless of the situation. On these visits, he would sometimes bring food items such as cooking oil, rice and corned beef. Whenever his well-tailored and expensive clothes needed ironing, he preferred that I handle the task, as I had almost perfected the art of giving clothes a long-lasting, neat press. One of my favourite possessions in the house was a hand-manual sewing machine. Whenever it malfunctioned, I would take it to an older gentleman near the central market who had excellent repair skills. If my uncle wasn't occupied with other tasks, he would often accompany me to the repairman, ensure a swift fix, and compensate him for the service.

On his part, Mum's uncle would usually spend time with his fellow peers from the teachers' training college, who resided on the other side of town. As a result, our home was always bustling with people coming and going. My Dad would return home in the evenings or late at night, only to leave early in the morning for work. Within the compound and the family, Mum held complete control over everything. During my earlier years, we lived in a rented house near the town centre, not far from the school, cinema and the market. However, there came a point when Mum decided to purchase a piece of land for the family. She approached the local Chief, called 'Alkalo,' a highly respected elderly man in his 80s who lived close to us. He was familiar with Mum and her intentions to acquire a piece of land after Mum asked him.

After my Mum learned about ongoing land distribution in a nearby area called Ebo Town, she applied for a plot of land. She was called upon. Mum and I with the Chief went to a huge space and measured the designated space using a measuring tape. Four poles were then placed on each corner to mark the demarcated boundaries of the land for Mum. The acquisition of this land was solely Mum's initiative, and Dad was unaware of it until later. I'm not certain when exactly he found out, but he chose to disregard the matter at first. As Mum began working at a peanut refinery factory in a place called Kanifing, located a 45-minute walk from home, she started saving money to develop the land. After a while, we constructed a three-room house and fenced the compound.

We spent a great deal of time at the new property, tending to the grass and making various repairs, treating it as if it were already home. Eventually, Mum decided it was time for us to move into our new place. However, Dad was hesitant and expressed his reluctance to relocate to a remote area as it was. As a child, I didn't fully understand his reasons, but Mum explained that he did not want to move away from the town centre. Mum's perspective was that owning a home is always preferable to renting, as the money spent on rent could be used for other purposes. There was likely a back-and-forth between them for several months. Finally, Mum decided for us to move to the new place, leaving Dad behind. We made the transfer and settled in, gradually adapting to the new environment and getting to know our new neighbours—without Dad. However, he eventually followed and moved in with us, and our family returned to a state of normalcy.

Although the distance between school and the market was greater, we grew accustomed to it over time. Owning a bicycle meant a great deal to me. I took meticulous care of it, regularly oiling, cleaning, and replacing parts as needed. Looking back, I recognize that Mum's strategic decision to acquire land for the family to live in, rather than continuing to rent, was the best gift parents could give their children. The freedom and space it provided us were invaluable. If we were still renting, I wouldn't have been able to cultivate my plants, flowers, poultry etc. Moving to the outskirts of town was a transformative experience.

The solitude and remote environment suited my character. The river was just a stone's throw away from home, surrounded by abundant natural beauty, mango trees, and various fruit-bearing trees. It was there that I began engaging in hunting activities, fishing, and swimming. After settling in, we noticed other new neighbours moving in as well. Soon, the entire area was filled with newcomers, and we found ourselves amid a growing community.

Throughout our journey from one rented residence to another, and finally, to our own home, we have always been fortunate to have friendly neighbours, except for one troublesome household. This family was constantly engaged in fights, quarrels, and verbal altercations, especially after drinking. As a young boy, I was afraid of them and took great care to avoid their compound.

In that compound, there was a young man who was probably around 20 years old at the time, though I hesitate to call him a man given his behaviour. He was constantly involved in fights, both with his siblings and with outsiders, often wielding broken bottles as weapons. I was extremely frightened of him and would always check outside to see if he was around before venturing out. The situation was more difficult, especially when you live opposite each other, just a stone's throw. That compound was plagued by constant yelling, profanity, and objects like stones, sticks and bottles thrown at each other, whether at night or daytime. The entire neighbourhood was held hostage by chaos and anarchy from that compound. Weekends were particularly dreadful, as they would get drunk and engage in never-ending fights.

Very early on, their youngest sister had been adopted by a Swedish family and taken to Sweden. During that time living in that rented house, there was a man who worked as a dispenser at the main Royal Victoria Hospital in Banjul. He owned a brand new Honda motorcycle, which was always parked in front of his door. He had a strong affinity for the Kora, a traditional 21-stringed musical instrument widely played in West Africa. He purchased a Kora and took private lessons then tried to teach me how to play. I managed to learn two songs on the instrument. This gentleman became somewhat of a saviour for us on occasions when my younger brother was out of control, whom I referred to as "the ultimate crier" The man would take him in, give him Horlicks or Ovaltine with milk to calm him down, then either put him to sleep or start playing the Kora for him and he would keep quiet.

We once also moved to a huge compound right in the heart of town, owned by an elderly lonely woman, which was conveniently located close to school and the market. The place was beautifully filled with the presence of at least 20 large mango trees. This attracted friends who would often come over to play with me to indulge in access to these mango trees. In front of the house, there was a wide sandy area where we would engage in various activities such as football, long jump, and high jump games, all done barefoot, resulting in our fair share of injuries. Among the residents of the compound, there was a young man, probably in his twenties, who never joined us in our games. He preferred to stay indoors, engrossed in his books, constantly studying. He would often assist me with my studies and treat me like a younger brother as our bond grew stronger. Having him as a mentor had a significant positive impact on me, as he exemplified calmness and composure.

Across the road from our compound, there was a lorry repair garage where trucks were parked all over the area, sometimes even outside our fence. The garage also had a dedicated welding area specializing in repairing lorry radiators, run by two brothers from Senegal. These brothers would frequently come over to our home, just opposite the garage, and request to have mangoes as if it had become a tradition! The younger brother among them owned a brand new men's Raleigh bicycle, but it was far too large for me to handle. However, he kindly took the time to teach me how to ride the bike, particularly during their less busy periods. It was under his guidance that I learned to ride a bicycle. I would position one foot and half of my body under the crossbar to the other side, and then start pedalling. People would often burst into laughter when they saw me, a small boy riding a big bicycle in such an unconventional manner. In that neighbourhood, there was also a man in his thirties who had mental health issues. He was always calm and spoke slowly, but unfortunately, the children in the area, including myself, would often torment him, teasing and making fun of him regularly.

The mentally ill man, despite his challenges, maintained a peaceful demeanour and never caused trouble for anyone. Although he was liked by everyone in the neighbourhood, he would often be seen talking to himself. One Sunday morning, when the garage was closed and a group of people, including the garage boss and the mentally ill man, gathered near our main gate, I playfully tickled the mentally ill man from behind, tickling his sides with both hands. In response, he let out a loud gas release, causing him to jump and turn back to the group, 'Did you hear that?' asking if we had heard the fart. This incident led to much laughter and mockery throughout the day. But the mentally ill man remained silent, never joining in the laughter or commenting further.

In Gambian society, there existed a prevalent belief in hearsay, superstitious beliefs, and unfounded stories. One such belief was that owls were considered evil birds, akin to witches, capable of causing harm to humans. There were large trees on the school grounds that housed owls, and children would engage in hunting and killing them. I, too, participated in these activities, joining a group of kids who would shout, run, kick, and throw stones at the unsuspecting owl. We believed that these birds possessed magical powers and were inherently evil. If I had known then what I know now about owls, I would have never taken part in those malicious activities against these magnificent creatures. The calmness of their flight, their round faces, and their striking eyes are among the admirable features that distinctly set them apart from other birds.

During the late sixties in The Gambia, the country had a relatively small population, and it was common for everyone to know each other. The community displayed a high level of politeness and courtesy towards one another. I recall greeting nearly everyone I encountered on the streets, whether I was familiar with them or not, and people would respond graciously. The road infrastructure at that time was quite poor. More than 90 per cent of the roads were made of red stones, while only a small portion of the road network was tarred. This inadequate infrastructure was a legacy of the colonial period, as the colonial masters had not invested much in developing the country's infrastructure. After ruling The Gambia for two hundred years, Britain had only established two hospitals, two high schools, and a few primary schools in the entire country.

Electricity supply was also scarce, but many families managed to cope with the situation. My uncle's place was located near the longest main road in the country, which stretched from the capital, Banjul, to the country's sole airport, passing through the Kombos in the southern part of the country and reaching Basse, the largest town in the far eastern part of the country known as the Upper River Region (URR). At that time, there were fewer vehicles on the road compared to today. Donkeys, cows, and horse carts were more commonly seen, capturing my attention as I would run outside to observe these animals carrying heavy loads. Loose animals such as sheep, dogs, pigs, and goats would roam freely on many streets. Many of the feeder roads were dirt roads with dusty stones and potholes, especially after the summer season.

Once upon a Saturday, my two friends and I found ourselves on the outskirts of the capital city, Banjul, eagerly waiting for a ride back home after an exhausting three-hour swimming session. We were tired and famished. Standing there, stranded for nearly an hour, we were growing increasingly desperate. Suddenly, a glimmer of hope appeared as one of my friends ecstatically exclaimed, "Hey, look! It's your Dad!" We thought our luck had turned around, believing that we would finally get the much-needed lift back home. With anticipation, I positioned myself prominently at the forefront, ensuring I would catch my Dad's attention. As he approached us from approximately fifty metres away, I began vigorously waving, hoping to establish eye contact. However, it soon became apparent that he wasn't slowing down, and there was no acknowledgement from him. Dad remained completely focused on the road, his gaze fixed only a couple of metres ahead of the bonnet. He seemed oblivious to everything else, including my waving and attempts to make myself visible.

I continued waving and shouting, "Pappa!" in a desperate bid to catch his attention, but he drove past us without even a glimpse. It was hard to fathom that Dad hadn't seen me waving at him. He maintained unwavering concentration, driving steadily forward. Disappointed and frustrated, we watched him slowly fade away into the distance. One of my friends couldn't contain his bewilderment and blurted out, "Boy, what happened?" To which I replied with a heavy heart, "He simply didn't see me." Eventually, we managed to secure a ride and made it back home. It was around seven in the evening when I finally arrived. I recounted the incident to my Dad, but all he could offer was a casual remark, "I didn't see you." Mum burst into laughter, remarking that when Dad is driving, his attention is solely fixated on the road, incapable of noticing anything else.

During a certain period, my Dad held the esteemed position of the chief driver at the renowned Wadner Beach Hotel, a favoured destination for Scandinavian tourists. This occupation came with its unique perks, particularly in the form of abundant food. Dad would bring home an array of culinary delights from the hotel, much to the delight of our neighbours and friends. There were fried chicken, cooked chicken, large tins of delectable blueberry and red-berry jam, bread, cheese, and even live European Red chickens of a special breed we affectionately referred to as Swedish chickens. These feathered additions are seamlessly integrated into my modest poultry collection. I would often carry copious amounts of bread and jam to school, sharing them with my friends or relishing the flavoursome combination during lunch breaks. With the surplus of bread, my resourceful Mum would ingeniously transform it into a nourishing treat. She would dry the bread, mix it with peanut butter and sugar, and pound it until it resembled couscous. This extraordinary concoction provided a satisfying and nutrient-rich sustenance, which not only increased water consumption but also curbed hunger due to the high-fat content of peanut butter, sugar, and dry bread.

One of the most exhilarating moments of the year was undoubtedly the Eid prayer celebrations. Schools would shut down for a minimum of two weeks in anticipation of the festivities. Each family would procure a ram to sacrifice on the auspicious day of Eid, resulting in a surplus of food and merriment shared with friends, relatives, and loved ones. Houses underwent extensive renovations and fresh coats of paint, while new carpets, curtains, and clothing were acquired for everyone. This period of Eid served as the pinnacle of income for tailors and various other traders. I vividly recall spending countless hours patiently awaiting my new clothes at the tailor during this bustling time. The actual day of Eid stood apart from all others. Every aspect of life was meticulously attended to; men and boys sported clean-shaven faces, while women and girls adorned themselves with meticulously styled hairdos or indulged in lengthy salon visits. Everyone presented their best selves, radiating happiness as they revelled in the festivities of the day.

For many, one of the most cherished moments of the day during Eid was the act of slaughtering a ram and relishing the taste of freshly grilled meat. After returning from the vast prayer ground, everyone gathered to perform collective prayers for approximately two hours.

At home, the aroma of cooking would fill the air as the ladies in every neighbourhood sped up to finish first. Particularly Mum would waste no time in preparing a delectable meal accompanied by the succulent grilled meat before any compound. The entire neighbourhood would come together to our house and partake in this communal feast. Year after year, Mum exhibited remarkable organizational skills and efficiency, ensuring she finished cooking before anyone else in our neighbourhood. We would then embark on a journey, moving from one household to another, enjoying the diverse array of lunches offered. Consequently, the unfortunate compound or person who finished cooking last would find their lunch uneaten, as everyone had already savoured multiple meals. Such camaraderie and harmonious collaboration among neighbours exemplified the spirit of our society.

However, as joyous as the occasion was, witnessing the actual slaughtering of the ram always proved to be the most challenging moment for me during the Eid period. It left me feeling despondent, and the haunting image lingered in my mind. This emotional impact was particularly profound when we had developed a bond with the ram, having cared for it by washing and feeding it for weeks, only to witness its life abruptly taken away. On Eid day, after enjoying a hearty lunch, everyone would adorn their new clothes and embark on a ceremonial tradition of acknowledging and expressing gratitude to one another. It was a time of festivity and unity. The younger children, donning their brand-new attire, would approach adults, seeking a small sum of money to purchase candy, a gesture steeped in tradition. There were numerous Eid celebrations when I had the pleasure of attending a live band show at the main cinema hall, just a short distance from home, which would last until around eight in the evening. Following the exhilarating performance, we would return home to indulge in a delightful dinner, capping off the day's festivities.

In the past, parties and celebrations would ensue throughout the night, spanning over a week. However, as a child, I never found myself drawn to or attended these festivities. They simply didn't capture my interest. Nevertheless, the vibrant celebrations continued, filling the air with joyous revelry.

One scorching day, when I was around fifteen years old, I encountered a remarkable sight on my way home from school. Amid an empty street, I stumbled upon an intense battle between a massive monitor lizard and a snake. Mesmerized, I stood there as the two creatures fiercely engaged in combat for what seemed like an eternity. After approximately five minutes, they abruptly decided to disengage and disappeared into the distance. This vivid scene left an indelible mark in my mind, forever etching a deep fear of snakes within me.

In Gambian culture, the extended family system is prevalent, with many households comprising numerous relatives. However, my immediate family consisted of only six children, relatively small compared to the average family size. As a homestay boy, my visits to relatives and loved ones residing in Banjul, Sere Kunda, or even in the countryside were infrequent.

Occasionally, some of our relatives would come to visit us, bringing warmth and familial connection into our home. Throughout that time, I have always found solace and comfort within the confines of our home, assisting Mum with various tasks or engaging in personal pursuits. School, on the other hand, was an environment that I wholeheartedly embraced. The activities, friendships, lessons, and the process of learning itself served as a constant source of stimulation and fulfilment. The surrounding wilderness boasted an abundance of mangoes and other fruits, freely accessible to anyone. During my regular walks to the nearby river, a mere kilometre away or a 15-minute stroll from home, I would often seize the opportunity to gather some mangoes along the way. The river, originating from Banjul, became a familiar retreat where I would frequently indulge in swimming. On occasion, I would venture further, finding a small canoe tied to the mangroves by local fishermen. Paddling through the flowing river, I would immerse myself in its tranquillity before returning the boat to its rightful place.

On one occasion, I embarked on my usual adventure, taking a canoe and venturing far out into the river. Little did I expect that this time would be different. As I was in the process of donning my nice clothes, an unfortunate mishap occurred—I lost my balance and plunged into the water. Despite my previous confidence and countless successful attempts, the unexpected happened, and I found myself submerged. The canoe was quickly filled with water, but I managed to swim with it until reaching shallow waters. Determined to salvage the situation, I decided to empty the water from the canoe by rocking it back and forth, allowing the water to gradually escape. This experience taught me a valuable lesson, and I never repeated such a daring feat. However, my visits to the river continued, primarily for swimming and fishing. My Mum, concerned about the potential dangers of drowning, expressed her wish for me to cease these excursions.

Unbeknownst to her, I possessed strong swimming abilities, and I regarded the river as less perilous than the sea. Around the age of 16, my interest in girls started to develop. I had a friend who was slightly older and lived near my home. After school, he would frequently visit, engaging in conversations about girls, love, and various other topics. It was through his influence and discussions that my interest in girls blossomed to the point where I gained the confidence to express my feelings to them. This friend had already gained experiences with girls that were quite different from my own. Living solely with his ailing Mum, who was unable to exercise discipline or control over his activities, he enjoyed a freedom that I had not yet experienced. He had the liberty to frequent dance clubs, something I had yet to venture into at that age. Interestingly, his elder brother happened to own a local dance club that operates on Friday, Saturday, and Sunday nights. This was where my friend would spend his evenings, engaging with different girls and participating in what is commonly known as "one-night stands." Such activities never crossed my mind, and I never felt compelled to visit his brother's dance club. It simply held no appeal to me.

As our friendship grew, my friend started spending more time with me, even joining us for meals. However, it became apparent that his main focus revolved around girls. It was during this period that I discovered he also smoked cigarettes, a habit that I disliked and had been advised by Mum to avoid. Concerned for his well-being, I urged him to quit smoking, and he made a promise to do so. To his credit, he always made sure not to smoke in my presence, which I appreciated. What truly set my friend apart was his incredible sense of humour. He was undoubtedly the funniest person I had ever encountered. His jokes had a vibrant and lively quality to them, capable of evoking laughter in even the most sombre and desolate individual. It seemed as though he possessed a natural gift for comedy, as he could effortlessly make people laugh uncontrollably. His talent extended beyond mere words, often incorporating physical actions and funny expressions into his performances. I had yet to come across a comedian who could match his level of skill.

I distinctly remember an incident when we had a visitor, an esteemed elderly gentleman who had come from the village to visit my Dad. He spent most of his time indoors, but he could hear my friend's jokes from outside. Little did we know that this well-respected visitor was thoroughly entertained by my friend's humour. One Saturday afternoon, after we had finished eating lunch, the gentleman emerged from the guest room and requested that I fetch my friend to share some jokes. To our surprise, this dignified visitor confessed to Mum that he greatly enjoyed listening to my friend's jokes, finding himself laughing continuously. He went on to express that he had never encountered anyone with such exceptional comedic storytelling abilities in his entire life. As our friendship progressed, I saw great potential in my friend's comedic talent and suggested that he consider pursuing a career as a comedian, drawing inspiration from the likes of Charlie Chaplin. Unfortunately, my well-intentioned suggestion did not sit well with him, and he became angry with me for making such a remark.

One of the most significant milestones in my romantic journey occurred when my first girlfriend, who happened to be my neighbour, came into my life. She was slightly older than me, but we attended different schools. Our relationship unfolded effortlessly since we had the opportunity to see each other daily. Adding to the connection, Mum was her Mum's closest friend, and our houses were conveniently located with just one compound separating us. I developed intense feelings for her, experiencing the thrill of my first love and romantic encounters. The desire to be in her presence consumed me, and I longed to spend every possible moment together. However, due to attending school in different locations, our interactions were limited to the evenings when we returned home as she would help with domestic work. This arrangement was far from satisfying. We decided to keep our relationship a secret, resorting to the exchange of clandestine love notes written on paper as there were no mobile phones at that time. Countless notes traversed between us during that period, fostering an atmosphere of mystery and excitement. The secrecy added a certain charm to our love, fuelling our motivation and intensifying our passion.

To maintain our covert relationship, we relied on her younger brother, who served as our trusted messenger, discreetly delivering the love notes between us. The thrill of this hidden romance was both exhilarating and challenging, enhancing the bond between us. Whenever we found ourselves alone, we would openly express our deep affection for one another. Sometimes, she would mention other individuals who showed interest in her, perhaps testing the extent of my jealousy. Among them was a cousin of mine who frequently visited us on weekends, persistently professing his admiration for her. However, I never confronted him about it, as I was confident in her unwavering devotion to me. I trusted her completely and took pride in the fact that she had chosen me above all others. Her love for me was palpable, and it filled me with a sense of self-worth. Our relationship blossomed over time, and we decided to take a significant step forward. We arranged for her to visit me in my small room, which served as a sort of pantry attached to the side of our large house. My room had a separate entrance accessible from the terrace, allowing her to enter without passing through the main house.

It seems that the suggestion for her to visit me in my room came about, but I cannot recall who exactly proposed the idea. Nevertheless, it was an enticing proposition that arrived a bit late in our relationship. Hence, we needed to devise a plan to make the visit possible. Both of our families consisted of about six to nine members, which could be considered a medium-sized family rather than a large one. In our respective homes, about five to six people were living permanently, including siblings and young children. This provided us with a suitable level of privacy, particularly with the availability of my little isolated pantry. The plan was for her to visit a relative in Brikama, a location outside of Sere Kunda where we lived, and then return home in the evening, passing through my place as I waited for her outside our compound.

The plan went smoothly, and she arrived around seven o'clock in the evening. Mum and everyone else, including the children, were in the main house, so we proceeded to my room without being noticed. This pattern of meeting each other became our norm, and we maintained a high level of discipline, control, and secrecy throughout. It was an arrangement that allowed us to spend time together while avoiding the watchful eyes of our families. My Mum would never have permitted me to have a girlfriend at such a young age. She prioritized my education and wanted to instil discipline and protect me, as any responsible and caring Mum would. Likewise, my girlfriend's Mum likely held similar concerns, as young girls are more vulnerable to the risks associated with early pregnancy. Despite the restrictions, our relationship grew more intense, romantic, and affectionate as we continued to find ways to be together.

As time went on, an unexpected twist shook our world: my girlfriend's Dad had arranged a marriage for her. The news hit us like a tidal wave, leaving us devastated and utterly powerless. We spent weeks grappling with the situation, desperately searching for a viable solution, but to no avail. It was during this tumultuous period that she suggested a daring plan - to flee to another bustling city, where we could seek refuge with distant relatives located a mere forty-five minutes away. However, I couldn't bring myself to embrace this idea, as it would mean severing ties with her Dad, an act I found hard to endorse. Another suggestion she put forward was to intentionally conceive a child, a proposition that I vehemently opposed.

My argument stemmed from my youthfulness and ongoing education, dreams and aspirations - becoming a Dad at such a tender age was simply not feasible. Moreover, the notion of her deliberately getting pregnant filled me with apprehension and alarm. Eventually, I made the difficult decision to end the relationship, realizing that continuing down this path might lead me down a road I wasn't prepared for - parenthood at such an early stage in life. Over time, our communication dwindled, and our once vibrant bond gradually faded away. Ultimately, we reached a poignant resolution: to comply with her Dad's wish for her to marry once she completed her education. The decision weighed heavily on us, fraught with challenges and sorrow. However, as life carried on, a sense of positivity and hope began to take root, guiding me towards a promising future.

I enthusiastically pursued my diverse array of interests, such as swimming and, more recently, taking up long-distance running in the evenings. In addition, I diligently tended to my beloved flowers, assisted my Mum with household chores, and took care of my poultry— all while maintaining my commitment to education. An emerging passion for football also captured my attention. After school, I would return to the grounds and engage in spirited practice sessions with teams, often returning home as late as seven in the evening. Engaging in physical and endurance training became a thrilling new pursuit, with running and playing football swiftly becoming my favourite activities. As a teenager, juggling these various endeavours kept me constantly occupied.

However, amidst my bustling routine, a compelling idea began to take root in my mind—a desire to venture abroad, particularly to the Western world. Although merely harbouring the thought did not offer a direct pathway to living overseas, listening to Radio Syd and watching Western movies further fuelled my aspiration of relocating to Europe. Embracing this notion, I began sharing my intentions with friends, expressing my desire to relocate to Europe. Regrettably, my statements were often met with laughter and mockery, as no one took them seriously. Yet, despite the challenges and the perceived unlikelihood of my dream materializing, the yearning to move to the West remained a prevalent aspiration in our small yet culturally rich country of The Gambia. As I previously mentioned, having a pen-friend from Scandinavia, or better yet, Europe, was considered fashionable and virtually every student had one or even two. For me, it became the ideal starting point for embarking on my journey.

In the past, we used to communicate by writing letters on special airmail paper that could be purchased from the general post office. These letters were sent abroad, and in return, we would receive replies through the post office. As young Gambians, we connected with pen pals and engaged in regular correspondence. It was our way of connecting with others, and in those days, it was our version of the internet. During that time, the country faced economic challenges, but despite the hardships, people made the most of what they had. There was a strong sense of community, where support was offered during both difficult and joyful times. Society, as a whole, embraced acceptance, affection, and harmony. Basic needs such as food, clothing, and access to healthcare were met for almost everyone.

As a teenager, I found myself in Scandinavia before I turned twenty. Surprisingly, I didn't experience the typical culture shock that people often talk about. Everything seemed familiar to me. Through movies, pictures, books, and communication with my pen-pal friends, I had already gained a good understanding of what Europe was like and how it looked.

I was aware that Scandinavia was known for its wealth, organization, sophistication, and advancements. Despite the cold weather, I believed it would be the ideal place for me to live. Back in the 70s, all that was required for entry into European countries was an airline ticket and a passport.

I had a secret pen-pal girlfriend who made a promise to help me secure admission to a college in Norway. Nobody, not even my family or close friends knew about this arrangement. It was strictly confidential and known only to me. I kept it hidden until I obtained my passport and ticket, and then I made the surprising announcement. The ticket I had was a round-trip ticket with a one-year validity. Even after a few people found out, I remained low-key and reserved, keeping things to myself. My Mum expressed worry and concern, as she felt I was too young and vulnerable. However, my Dad remained silent, not offering any response except to say, "Let him go, he is a man, and if you don't like it there, just come back."

While my Mum was more anxious, she also recognized that going to Scandinavia presented a once-in-a-lifetime opportunity for a successful future. She spoke about it incessantly, offering advice and guidance. She emphasized that if conditions became unfavourable, I must return home. Her best friend also offered me advice, urging me to behave well and stay away from trouble. She mentioned that my Mum was so worried about me that she even shed tears. In response, I reassured her, just as I had assured my Mum, that I would always steer clear of trouble and commotion. I emphasized that my primary focus was on education and personal growth.

Chapter 2

Life In Sweden, Scandinavia

T he opportunity to study in Norway and the availability of scholarships, particularly for African students, became widely known among students in The Gambia. The prospect of studying in Norway and pursuing a career as a marine biologist captured everyone's imagination. The topic of Norwegian scholarships became a popular conversation, and for me, having a pen pal from Norway became a beacon of hope.

With my passport and a return ticket in hand, heading to Norway felt like winning a million-dollar lottery. As I embarked on my journey, I flew to Denmark and arrived at Kastrup International Airport in the early hours of the morning, around 03:00 a.m.

The airport appeared vast and significantly more advanced compared to what I was accustomed to back home, but there were only a few people around. I went through passport control and customs checks, and I noticed a group of taxi drivers gathered nearby. Following the instructions given to me by my girlfriend, I inquired about the trains. I boarded a train to Copenhagen Central Station, which took less than thirty minutes. There, I waited until around 06:00 a.m. for the next train to Stockholm.

While waiting for the train to Stockholm, I enjoyed some peanuts I had with me and used the opportunity to exchange one of my three traveller's cheques, each worth a hundred dollars. After satisfying my hunger, I boarded the train and made my way to Stockholm, Sweden.

Instead of proceeding directly to Norway, I decided to spend a few days exploring Stockholm. In the heart of Stockholm, at a fast-food restaurant, I encountered an African (who later became a good friend) who greeted me with a friendly "hello." Curiously, I asked him if any Gambians were living in Stockholm. To my delight, he replied, "Oh yes, I am a Gambian. I can give you a telephone number you can call." He directed me to a place called the Gambian Club, where Gambians gathered regularly. It was a pleasant surprise that the first black person I met and conversed with in Stockholm happened to be a fellow Gambian.

During my stay in Stockholm, I resided in a student hostel that I had booked in advance, planning to continue my journey to Norway afterwards. As it was October, the autumn season brought about a slightly cold climate. I dialled the given telephone number and received directions to the Gambian Club. Around nine in the evening, I arrived at the club, and to my surprise, I encountered several individuals whom I already knew from The Gambia. It was not unusual considering the small size of our home country and how closely connected people were, often through mutual acquaintances. Interestingly, I even discovered that a cousin whom I believed to be living in Holland had met a Swedish woman and moved to Sweden, unbeknownst to me. He was a member of a music group that I thought had gone on a tour to Holland, but life had taken a different turn for him.

We greeted each other warmly with genuine excitement and emotions running high. It had been years since we last saw each other, and there was a strong sense of reunion. My cousin, overwhelmed by the joy of our encounter, immediately suggested that I retrieve my belongings from the hostel and move into their apartment in the eastern centre of Stockholm, where he resided with his girlfriend. I mentioned my plans to go to Norway and the prepaid three-day stay at the hostel, but he was adamant and insisted that I stay with them for a few days. Eventually, I gave in to his persistence, and we took a taxi to collect my belongings before heading to his apartment.

The following day, after having lunch together, my cousin proposed that we visit his friend on the other side of town. After the visit, coming home, we rushed to catch the train, almost missing it, and found vacant seats upon boarding. As the train departed the station, a young, fair-skinned girl with blonde hair took a seat directly across from me. She locked eyes with me, offering a friendly smile from a distance of less than half a metre. Naturally, I returned the smile, engaging pleasantly. Sensing an inquisitiveness in the air, my cousin playfully suggested in our language, Wollof, that I speak to her to gauge her reaction. Taking his advice, I struck up a conversation with her, and to my surprise, she displayed great interest in me when I mentioned that I had just arrived in Stockholm the previous day. She enthusiastically declared that she would be the one to show me around the city!

The girl's name was Annie, and she happened to be a 19-year-old student like myself. Despite the short duration of our train conversation, it was incredibly enjoyable and meaningful. Annie generously offered me her phone number and requested that I call her. True to my word, I contacted her that Sunday, and she expressed curiosity about the address of my current residence. After sharing the details, I discovered that she lived just two train stops away from my cousin's place where I was staying. I was taken aback when she proposed picking me up and inviting me for a coffee session at her home. Excitedly, I accepted her invitation. Around six in the evening, Annie arrived at my cousin's place, and we embarked on a short train ride to her residence, which was less than ten minutes away. Little did I know that this evening would lead to a profound bond between us. We spent the night together, engaging in heartfelt conversations and sharing intimate moments until dawn.

Annie revealed that she was studying economics at university and that her parents resided in Vasteras, approximately over an hour's drive away from Stockholm. We decided to gather my belongings from my cousin's place the following day, and in a significant turn of events, Annie and I chose to live together. She became not only my lover but also my best friend and most cherished companion. My encounter with Annie became an unexpected obstacle on my journey to Norway. I found myself deeply in love with her and decided to stay in Stockholm. As a result, my ticket to Oslo, Norway was cancelled, along with the three-day hostel booking I had made upon my arrival in Stockholm. Love had altered my path, and Annie became the reason for my choice to remain in the city.

Our two-room flat near Saint Eriksplan, right in the centre of Stockholm, offered us a convenient and vibrant living environment. The area was brimming with amenities, museums, bustling stores, and various forms of entertainment, including one of the city's most popular clubs. I quickly realized that Annie was an incredibly sociable and well-liked individual, with a wide circle of friends. Her openness and outgoing nature made her someone everyone wanted to get to know. Gradually, her friends started visiting our place, and on weekends, we occasionally organized small house parties. It felt like a comfortable and familiar home for me. Annie expressed surprise at my organized, calm, and detail-oriented nature. She held my attitude in high regard, often emphasizing her desire to be more like me. Inspired by our relationship, she sought to mirror my openness, show genuine interest in others, extend kindness to all, and develop the ability to listen and understand people.

She enthusiastically shared with everyone, including her parents, how well-suited I was for her. I swiftly became ingrained and integrated within her circle, interacting with outgoing, ambitious, and resourceful individuals and colleagues. As a teenager who had recently arrived from the small Gambia just weeks ago, I found myself observing the stark contrast between my previous life and the warm reception I received from the Swedes. They treated me with kindness and friendliness, eager to learn about my experiences, feelings, and thoughts, and eager to delve into discussions about Africa, its diverse cultures, and rich traditions. Living in Sweden proved to be an immense change for me, both climatically and culturally, opening up new opportunities for growth and understanding.

Our group of young individuals shared a common belief that we could bring about change in the world from the grassroots level. Each of us had our passions and interests: some were driven by political ambitions, others were dedicated to tackling climate change, while some advocated for human rights and injustices. Amidst this diverse range of ideologies, I found myself in the midst of it all, actively participating, engaging in debates, and contributing to the formulation of political ideologies. We eagerly conversed, canvassed door-to-door, and spoke to as many people as possible to spread our message and gather support. Annie's friends, many of whom were university students, shared this passion for change and actively pursued their ideals. Our group never engaged in the consumption of alcohol, drugs, or cigarettes, aligning perfectly with my comfort zone. I had never desired or planned to partake in such activities, and it was reassuring to be in an environment where they were not present.

Annie herself was an overconfident and self-assured individual, involved in multiple activities simultaneously. She dedicated her time to the humanitarian party as her full-time political ambition, worked part-time, and even attended ballet classes, among other commitments. Her remarkable ambition and unwavering seriousness in everything she undertook inspired me. I wholeheartedly supported her endeavours, accompanying her as we distributed political flyers, organized meetings and workshops, and attended gatherings with our friends. Together, we sought to make a difference and contribute to creating a better world. Our shared passion for activism and our collective efforts brought us closer as we navigated through the challenges and joys of pursuing our ideals.

My culinary skills and knack for organization honed back home, proved to be valuable assets that were appreciated by everyone around me. I was adept at cooking ample amounts of food, including salads and sandwiches, which could sustain Annie and me for several days. Whenever friends dropped by feeling hungry, I made sure they never left without a satisfying meal. Keeping a steady supply of ready-to-eat food became a priority, and we often enjoyed vegetable soups with bread and salads. Additionally, I took charge of organizing grocery shopping and ensuring that our apartment remained clean and well-arranged, skills that I had already mastered in the Gambia. Financially, I didn't have substantial funds with me.

However, I managed to support myself with personal hygiene items like soap, toothpaste, and toothbrushes, and occasionally I would cover the costs of grocery shopping. Although I never asked for or accepted money from others, some of the people I knew displayed tremendous kindness and generosity towards me. Their support was invaluable. In terms of assimilating into society, I effortlessly fit in and quickly became a part of the community. I had numerous friends, engaging activities, and a wide range of interests that kept me consistently busy. It felt as though I had been living in Stockholm for years. I navigated the city using public transportation, becoming familiar with both the underground and bus systems. I mastered the connections and various parts of Stockholm, allowing me to easily travel from one side of the city to the other.

Annie and I shared a love for dining out, particularly in the Southside of town known as Skanstull and Slussen. This area was home to a variety of fantastic small restaurants and cafes, situated on higher ground, offering breathtaking views of Stockholm from above. The summer season was the perfect time to visit these establishments, as the daylight stretched late into the evening, creating magical scenes and atmosphere. One evening, after a few months of living in Stockholm, Annie returned from her lectures with a paper registration receipt for a three-day writer's course. To my surprise, she had registered me without prior discussion. I questioned why she hadn't informed me before before paying for the registration.

Despite my initial reluctance, Annie remained firm in her belief that the course would be beneficial and suited my interests in writing. She emphasized that I did have good writing skills especially the poems I wrote for her, and thought I could be a good writer. Her final response didn't waver: "I paid for it because I know how creative you are and that you have the potential to be a great writer. Attending this course is the right choice for you." I kept quiet and accepted. Her unwavering confidence convinced me to give it a try. The course was conducted in English by a literature professor from Cambridge University. On the first day, I attended the course alone, registering my name at the door and finding a seat in the middle of a filled hall. The room was buzzing with anticipation, as attendees eagerly awaited the course to begin.

On the first day, we delved into the use of active verbs, honing our skills in sentence formulation and creative writing. These lessons seamlessly carried over to the following day. As Sunday arrived, we reached the culmination of our learning journey. Each of us had the task of presenting a piece of writing, on any subject of our choosing, which had to be read aloud before the entire class.

I meticulously crafted a poem, encompassing three-quarters of a page, employing concise and impactful sentences. Before my turn to present, I took the opportunity to revise my work. However, as the anticipation grew and my peers stepped forward one by one, nerves and anxiety began to manifest.

Beads of sweat formed on my forehead, witnessing their performances accompanied by applause and remarks from the professor. I swiftly skimmed through my composition once more, realizing that my turn was rapidly approaching. Time seemed to accelerate, and suddenly, it was my moment to shine at the front. Standing before approximately a hundred individuals, whom I had only met three days prior, I prepared to share my creation.

With confidence radiating from within, I gracefully strode towards the podium, ascending the platform for the very first time. The sight of so many faces and the grand setting instilled a sense of awe. Sporting a wide smile, I greeted the audience and the professor with a resounding, motivating voice, eliciting an enthusiastic response from the entire hall. Succinctly summarizing the essence of my poem, I unveiled its title.

As I began reciting my poem, the nervousness I felt started to dissipate. I spoke with clarity and confidence, projecting my voice to reach every corner of the hall. Each line flowed smoothly, punctuated by pauses and emphasis where necessary. The words resonated with emotion and meaning, capturing the essence of my thoughts and feelings.

As I reached the final stanza, the atmosphere in the room seemed to change. The audience leaned in, hanging onto every word. The power of my words and their impact on the listeners became evident. The room fell silent as I concluded the poem, leaving a brief moment of reflection before the applause erupted.

The applause was thunderous, and the smiles and nods from fellow participants filled me with a sense of accomplishment. The professor commended my writing, praising the imagery, the rhythm, and the depth of emotion conveyed through my words.

I beamed with pride as I returned to my seat, knowing that I had successfully shared a piece of my creativity and connected with an audience. The experience of presenting my work in front of a large audience boosted my confidence as a writer and reaffirmed Annie's belief in me. It was a transformative moment that inspired me to continue exploring my passion for writing and expressing myself through words. I found myself once more at the forefront, where I was tasked with an improvisation. Feeling a surge of adrenaline, I took a deep breath and allowed my mind to flow freely. The words began to form in my thoughts, and I started to speak, weaving a spontaneous poem that emerged from the depths of my creativity. Each line unfolded naturally, guided by my emotions and the energy in the room.

As I continued, the words flowed effortlessly, carrying meaning and capturing the essence of the moment. The audience remained captivated, hanging onto every word as they witnessed the birth of a poem in real-time. The rhythm and cadence of my improvised verses resonated with the listeners, evoking a range of emotions and painting vivid imagery in their minds. When I reached the final lines, the room erupted in applause once again. The professor, visibly impressed, commended the spontaneity and depth of my improvisation.

The audience showered me with praise and admiration, their applause reverberating through the hall. I stood there, amazed and humbled by the response. It was a moment of pure artistic expression, a testament to the power of the written and spoken word. The experience ignited a newfound confidence in my ability to create and connect through poetry, and it left an indelible mark on my journey as a writer.

The room fell into a hushed silence, a reverent pause after the storm of applause. I stood there, basking in the moment, feeling the energy of the audience still lingering in the air. It was a moment of pure exhilaration, a culmination of raw emotion and artistic expression. As I made my way back to my seat, I could sense the impact of my improvised poem resonating with those who had listened. The room was filled with a palpable sense of awe and admiration as if we had all been swept away by the power of the spoken word. The professor, beaming with pride, took a moment to collect his thoughts before addressing the class. He spoke of the beauty of spontaneous creation, the ability to tap into the depths of one's creativity and share it with the world. He praised my courage, my willingness to take risks and trust in my abilities.

The audience, still buzzing with excitement, showered me with kind words and gestures of appreciation. Strangers approached me, expressing their admiration and gratitude for the emotions I had evoked within them. It was a humbling experience, a reminder of the profound impact that art can have on people's lives. At that moment, I felt a deep sense of fulfilment and purpose.

I realized that poetry was not just a hobby or a pastime; it was a language of the soul, a means of connecting with others on a profound level. I had discovered a gift within myself, one that I would continue to nurture and explore in the years to come. Leaving the stage that day, I carried with me the echoes of applause, the memories of a transformative experience. I had found my voice, and I knew that it was only the beginning of a lifelong journey as a poet, a storyteller, and a purveyor of the human experience through the power of words.

The room erupted in a frenzy of excitement and admiration as I concluded my improvised poem. The audience was captivated by the imagery and emotions woven into my words. Applause thundered through the hall, reverberating off the walls, mingling with cheers and shouts of appreciation. The professor stood before me, a mix of amazement and delight on his face. He marvelled at my ability to conjure such heartfelt verses on the spot. His words of encouragement resonated deeply within me, and I felt a surge of inspiration coursing through my veins. As the applause subsided, the professor addressed the class once again, singling me out as an example of untapped potential. He urged me, and all those present, to embrace our creativity and embrace the power of writing. He emphasized that there was no need to wait for the perfect moment or the ideal circumstances, but to seize the present and let our voices be heard.

Receiving the Writer's Prize, a symbol of recognition and validation, filled me with a sense of pride and determination. It was a tangible reminder of the talent and passion that lay dormant within me, waiting to be unleashed onto the blank pages of countless stories and poems. Grateful for the support and encouragement of those around me, I thanked the audience, the professor, and my fellow participants. Their belief in my abilities fuelled my confidence and affirmed my decision to embark on a writing journey. Leaving the course that day, clutching the Writer's Prize in my hands, I felt a renewed sense of purpose and direction. The professor's words echoed in my mind, propelling me forward, and urging me to embrace my passion and share my stories with the world.

From that moment on, I would no longer wait for the right time or the perfect opportunity. I would seize the pen, wield the power of words, and embark on a lifelong quest to capture emotions and touch the hearts of others through my writing. The course had ignited a fire within me, and I was determined to let it burn bright, illuminating the path of my literary journey.

As I returned to my seat, surrounded by the warmth of applause, I couldn't help but feel a sense of fulfilment and gratitude. I had not only shared my written work but also offered a glimpse into the realm of spontaneous creation. It was a moment that would stay with me, reminding me of the boundless possibilities of expression and the transformative power of words.

It was a joyous occasion as I returned home, eager to share the news of my success with Annie. I couldn't contain my excitement as I showed her the Writer's Prize and recounted the events of the course. Her pride and happiness mirrored my own, and she wasted no time in spreading the word to our loved ones. Annie made phone calls to her parents, friends, and sister, relaying the story of my achievement with enthusiasm. The news spread like wildfire, and soon our home was filled with friends who came to celebrate and offer their congratulations.

The atmosphere was lively, with laughter, cheers, and words of encouragement filling the air. It was an overwhelming display of support, and I felt grateful for the genuine camaraderie and belief in my writing abilities. A few days later, a large envelope arrived, containing a congratulatory letter signed by all the participants of the course. Each person shared their thoughts on my poems, highlighting their favourites and encouraging me to pursue writing further. The heartfelt words touched me deeply, and I treasured the letter as a testament to the impact my words had made on those around me.

In response to this outpouring of support, I expressed my gratitude to Annie for her unwavering belief in me. Her insistence on me taking the course proved to be a turning point in my life. She had seen my potential even before I fully realized it myself, and her faith in my abilities was instrumental in my success. Motivated by this newfound validation and support, I wasted no time enrolling in a language school to learn Swedish. I recognized the importance of mastering the language to fully immerse myself in the culture and connect with the Swedish community on a deeper level. While I had already learned some words and basic sentence structures, I was determined to expand my linguistic skills and express myself fluently in my new home.

The journey to becoming proficient in Swedish was an exciting challenge, complementing my growing passion for writing. It opened doors to further communication and understanding, allowing me to engage with a wider audience and share my stories and experiences more effectively. With Annie by my side, supporting and encouraging me every step of the way, I embarked on this new chapter in my life. The future was brimming with possibilities, and I was filled with anticipation for the adventures yet to come. Completing language school with excellent marks within a couple of months was a significant achievement for me. I embraced the learning process wholeheartedly, with my trusty Swedish dictionary as my constant companion.

The willingness and dedication to learn the language, coupled with the support of my friends and Swedish girlfriend, made it easier for me to practise and immerse myself in Swedish culture. It amazed many people how well I spoke the language, considering my relatively short time in the country. Stockholm City, the vibrant and lively capital, never failed to captivate me. It was a place brimming with energy and diversity, attracting tourists from all corners of the globe. Live band tours would grace various venues, and the city's restaurants were filled with a zestful atmosphere, serving delicious food and coffee. What impressed me the most was the city's ability to maintain order and cleanliness, which was rarely seen to such an extent elsewhere.

During the winter months, indoor concerts provided entertainment, allowing people to gather and enjoy music despite the challenging weather. However, it was during the summer when Stockholm truly came alive with large outdoor concerts and performances. Many renowned bands, groups, and artists would visit the city, providing unforgettable experiences for music enthusiasts like myself. I had the opportunity to attend concerts by legendary artists such as Michael Jackson, Stevie Wonder, Janet Jackson, Youssou Ndour, R. Kelly, Ray Charles, Whitney Houston, Jennifer Lopez, the Senegalese National Troupe, Usher, Ravi Shankar, Lionel Richie, and many more. The range of talent and musical genres was truly remarkable, creating a rich and diverse cultural tapestry. From pop icons to soulful singers, from international sensations to local talents, Stockholm offered a vibrant music scene that catered to a variety of tastes.

Attending these concerts was an incredible privilege, and each performance left a lasting impression on me. The city's ability to attract high-profile artists and host world-class concerts was a testament to its cultural significance and the enthusiasm of its residents and visitors. It added another layer of excitement and richness to my experience in Stockholm, contributing to the memories I cherished of my time there. Indeed, Sweden has a vibrant music scene that has contributed to its reputation as a musical country. From popular international artists to local Swedish bands, there is a wide range of musical talent that flourishes within the country. Artists like Europe, Dr Alban, Lena Philipsson, Jerry Williams, Roxette, Ace of Base, and many more have made their mark on the Swedish music scene. Music education is highly valued in Sweden, with children learning music in primary school and people of all ages participating in choirs and musical activities.

This emphasis on music from a young age has helped foster a culture of musical talent and appreciation throughout the country. It's no wonder that Sweden is the third-largest music-producing country globally, after the USA and the UK, generating substantial revenue for the nation each year. Sweden's musical landscape encompasses a wide range of genres and styles. Reggae concerts, jazz festivals, dance bands, and open-air concerts attract enthusiastic audiences in various locations. The accessibility to bands and groups allows for a diverse and thriving music culture not only in Stockholm but also across the entire country. The success of Swedish music extends beyond the borders, with talented producers and songwriters like Max Martin and Denniz Pop attracting prominent international artists. Their collaborations with artists such as Britney Spears, Backstreet Boys, Westlife, Madonna, Ace of Base, and many others have resulted in chart-topping hits that have made a significant impact on the global music scene.

The influence of Swedish music goes beyond its artistic and cultural significance. It has played a crucial role in Sweden's socioeconomic system, generating substantial revenue and contributing to the country's overall economy. Iconic Swedish groups like ABBA and Roxette have helped bring Sweden closer to people worldwide and have left a lasting impact on popular music. As I continued to explore Stockholm and Sweden, I had the opportunity to immerse myself in various activities, from skiing trips to attending meetings and conferences. The cultural and musical offerings in and around Stockholm and throughout the country provided me with a wealth of experiences and further enriched my time in Sweden.

In the early 80s, I decided to join a language course offered at ABF Sveavagen, conveniently located in the town centre. It was a full-time commitment, with classes scheduled for four hours a day, five days a week. I had made the necessary payments in advance, ensuring my enrolment was secured. At that time, receiving a monthly stipend of approximately four thousand kronor while pursuing my studies seemed like a favourable arrangement. With my ambition set on staying in Sweden, I proceeded to apply for a residential and working permit. Fortunately, the application process went smoothly, and I obtained all the required documents within a few weeks. Three years later, I found myself contemplating the idea of obtaining a Swedish passport. Surprisingly, the application procedure was relatively quick, and I soon held a Swedish passport in my hands.

One pleasant day, my girlfriend presented me with an intriguing proposal. She suggested that we take a break from our studies and embark on a journey to live in and explore the United States together. Initially, I had reservations about this idea, but I eventually decided to embrace it. Relationships are built on sacrifice, compromise, and reciprocity, so I agreed with her proposition. We diligently saved a significant portion of our monthly earnings, and our destination of choice became California. We initially settled in Sonoma County and later moved to Monte Rio. Throughout our time in California, we embarked on various adventures, exploring renowned locations such as Los Angeles, Disneyland, Hollywood, the San Diego Zoo, and SeaWorld, as well as venturing to Nevada to visit Reno and Las Vegas. While in the United States, I took the opportunity to enrol in an Advanced English course at Berkeley University. However, due to the nature of our travels and experiences, I could only manage to attend a few classes.

Unfortunately, I was unable to complete the course before we departed from the US. Although we met some acquaintances during our stay, our social circle primarily consisted of friends of my girlfriend's friends. Regrettably, I must admit that my personal experience of living in the US did not bring me the level of enjoyment I had anticipated. Discrimination, particularly by law enforcement, was alarmingly prevalent during my time in the United States, despite my earnest efforts to abide by the rules of the day. I frequently found myself subjected to unjust treatment, whether it was on the road, in shopping malls, or even when attempting to enter a respectable restaurant or club. It was a constant reminder of the humiliation, distress, and fear that discrimination brings, especially when it jeopardizes my safety.

Over time, the toll of such experiences wears me down, leading to a withdrawal from places where I knew I am unwelcome or likely to face discrimination, all to protect my dignity. And when prejudice is encountered in front of my loved ones or friends, the sense of humiliation is only magnified. After spending approximately a year in the United States, the most important decision for me was to relinquish my stay and return home to Sweden. These two countries stand in stark contrast to each other when it comes to societal norms and lifestyle. The people in the United States tend to be more outgoing but can also be brusque and informal, whereas, in Sweden, individuals are generally more reserved, introverted, and formal. I identify more with the latter category. With this realization, we chose to leave the United States behind and make our way back to Stockholm. It was a homecoming eagerly awaited by our friends and my partner's family, who were eager to reunite with us, hear our stories, and see the photographs documenting our journey.

Upon our return, I decided to secure a full-time job while continuing my self-taught lessons at home. Meanwhile, my partner chose to resume her studies, prioritizing her commitments to achieve a more balanced and fulfilling life. Learning from our past experiences, she decided to let go of dance classes, and political activities, and reduce the number of close friends. This shift allowed us to focus on building a stable foundation for our relationship and develop short and medium-term plans for our future together. Our time in the United States was marked by exploration and discovery. While adjusting to our new routine, we also made sure to find time to visit friends and maintain those connections.

In addition, I brought along second-hand books from Berkeley University's school library, enabling me to continue correspondence in Advanced English with the university. Juggling our various responsibilities, we had plenty on our plates. Despite our best efforts, financial constraints prevented us from indulging in extravagant activities. Every outing had to be carefully planned, taking into account the associated costs, whether it was visiting museums, enjoying family funfairs, exploring the San Diego Zoo, experiencing Disneyland and Hollywood, or embarking on a trip to Reno, Nevada, and other destinations. Returning to our two-room flat with the security of a full-time job brought a sense of relief, even though my unwavering desire and admiration for Stockholm remained intact.

However, our visits to certain public clubs on weekends often led to disappointments and let-downs. These experiences served as reminders that not all aspects of our home city lived up to our expectations, despite our strong attachment to it. Frequenting clubs and occasionally joining my partner and her friends, I often encountered difficulties when attempting to enter these establishments as a black man. These clubs were well-known in the town, sometimes hosting artists primarily from the United States, or simply functioning as a disco with a restaurant. Unfortunately, the club discrimination I faced in the United States seemed to persist in Sweden as well. The clubs would cite dress codes or request membership cards, even in places where such requirements were unnecessary.

Discrimination against blacks and other ethnic minorities attempting to enter these clubs became increasingly prevalent, even though it is illegal. However, proving such discrimination in a court of law proved to be challenging, which is why many black individuals choose not to pursue legal action against these clubs. Interestingly, when my partner Annie, who is white, or her all-white friends would accompany me, they would effortlessly gain access to any club or restaurant without being questioned about membership cards. However, whenever I was stopped from entering, it would often lead to outbursts of anger from my partner and friends, resulting in chaos at the entryway.

Eventually, we would either gain entry or decide to leave the premises altogether. The practice of requesting membership cards in cases where they are not required is a means to prevent black individuals from entering these clubs. Many people of foreign-born or dark-skinned backgrounds have grown frustrated with this discriminatory practice. There have been instances where even a member of parliament, accompanied by a visiting foreign ambassador, was denied access to a restaurant due to discrimination. An unfortunate incident occurred that garnered widespread attention when our Prime Minister expressed his frustration over Sweden's reputation being tarnished as a racist country due to incidents of club discrimination. Some club owners found themselves defending their actions in court, but ultimately, no significant changes were made. I recall a black BBC journalist who came to Stockholm after hearing about the difficulties faced by black individuals when trying to enter clubs or restaurants.

He experienced the same issue, being denied access after attempting to dine at a couple of establishments in the old town, of Gamla Stan. While his friends faced no such barriers, he was the only one who asked for a membership card. This incident made headlines on the BBC as well as in Sweden. Several prominent politicians have openly expressed their shame and disgust regarding this discriminatory practice, yet little has been done to rectify the issue of club and restaurant discrimination. For me, club discrimination was a minor aspect of my life. I refused to allow it to affect me, but it did lead me to avoid certain clubs and restaurants where I was certain discrimination would occur. The practice itself is humiliating.

However, there are numerous aspects of Stockholm that I adore beyond the club scene. As time passed, clubs for Blacks began to emerge, offering a more inclusive atmosphere and celebrating a diverse range of cultures, regardless of whether individuals were black or white. The music in these clubs was often better, and soon enough, they became popular destinations for people of all backgrounds. After spending some time working and pursuing self-study, I decided to enrol part-time in a college called Komvux in Stockholm. There, I focused on the advanced Swedish language and mathematics. Komvux serves as a college-level institution for adults, offering individuals a second chance to further their education. It is a valuable system that helps many people, particularly those aiming to pursue higher education.

In the mid-80s, my partner, her best friend, and I embarked on a memorable summer holiday adventure. We decided to drive to Spain, passing through Germany and France. This journey covered a distance of over 3,000 kilometres and took us a day and a half. It was filled with joy, breathtaking sightseeing, and endless amusement, making it one of my best holidays ever. Upon our arrival in Granada, Spain, late in the evening, we checked into a motel for the night. The following morning, we enjoyed a hearty breakfast, freshened up, changed our clothes, and set out to explore Torremolinos.

We spent time at the beach, wandered around the area, and later indulged in a delightful dinner. We visited iconic landmarks such as Alhambra, the Palace of Charles V, and Palacio de Generalife, immersing ourselves in the rich history and beauty of the region. Inspired by the success and fulfilment of our initial trip, we decided to repeat the journey multiple times. There was even a year when seven friends expressed their desire to join us, although we could only accommodate two of them, one of whom was Annie's elder sister. These trips created lasting memories and further strengthened the bonds of friendship and adventure among us. Exploring Spain by car and immersing ourselves in its various attractions proved to be a somewhat expensive adventure. The weather was consistently pleasant, and we were spoiled with an abundance of delicious food.

Everywhere we went, we encountered a plethora of historical and modern sights to behold. In the mid-80s, the clubs in Spain were unparalleled, unrivalled by any other location worldwide. Surprisingly, I never encountered club discrimination during our time in Spain. Instead, I found myself in a peculiar situation where girls would occasionally vie for my attention, even in the presence of my partner! On one occasion, we visited a club in Zeneta, Murcia around 1:00 am. The club was bustling with people, and upon arrival, it was customary to receive a complimentary drink by presenting your ticket at the bar. After obtaining our drinks, we made our way to a table at the back of the dancehall, comfortably engaging in conversation about our surroundings.

Suddenly, a beautiful and slender girl approached us, asking for a dance. Annie looked at me with a broad smile and jokingly said, "Go ahead and dance, but behave yourself." However, amid our dance, another girl abruptly inserted herself between us, grabbing hold of my hand.

The scene at the club in Zeneta, Murcia escalated quickly as the first girl shouted in Spanish, "Que haces?!" Él es mi Moreno!» (What are you doing? He›s my Blackman!) She forcefully pushed the other girl, causing her to fall to the floor amidst the dancing crowd.

The girl got up and retaliated by slapping her, resulting in a brief scuffle before the guards intervened and separated them. We later discovered that the second girl was the daughter of the club owner.

During another outing in Torrevieja, we decided to visit a renowned nightclub. Late into the night, a gentleman approached me and introduced himself as the club owner. Annie was hesitant and advised against engaging with him, expressing concerns about my safety, and with the loud music inside communication was unclear. Despite her reservations, we agreed to step outside with the guy, who eventually introduced himself as the club owner, a man in his forties with a beard. Once outside, introduced himself again in broken English and expressed his suspicion that we were not residents but rather tourists.

We confirmed that we were indeed from Sweden, enjoying our holiday. To our surprise, the man proposed that I become a DJ at his club for two weekends. We couldn't help but burst into uncontrollable laughter. I informed the man that I had never been a DJ before. However, he insisted that if I were to come to the club the following day, someone would teach me the ropes for a couple of hours.

He also assured me that the hourly rate he was willing to pay me would exceed what he paid his other DJs. It was an unexpected and amusing proposition that left us all shaking with laughter. After discussing it with Annie, we ultimately decided to accept the club owner's request.

We made plans to return the following weekend to fulfil the DJ job. The next day, I underwent a four-hour training session from 2 PM to 6 PM to familiarize myself with the DJ equipment and techniques.

Afterwards, we enjoyed a nice dinner before embarking on my first-ever DJ gig. The job involved seamlessly transitioning between songs, mixing tracks, ensuring compatibility, and knowing when and where to adjust the volume to create a smooth overlap, all while keeping the dance floor lively and energetic. To Annie's surprise, I performed exceptionally well, consistently keeping the dance floor packed with enthusiastic partygoers. It was an unforgettable adventure that feels as vivid today as it did back then.

According to Pedro, the club owner, he simply wanted to showcase a black man as a DJ, given that black artists were responsible for much of the music we listen to and dance to. He enthusiastically captured numerous pictures of me in the DJ booth, wearing oversized headphones.

I never found out what became of those pictures. Nevertheless, the holiday trip, coupled with two weeks of DJ work, marked the end of my short-lived DJ career.

Spain quickly became our preferred holiday destination, as we found the Spanish people to be warm-hearted, delightful, and attractive, and the food simply delicious.

During one of our trips to Spain, we had the opportunity to attend an incredible concert in Madrid at the Plaza de Toros featuring renowned artists like Julio Iglesias and Miguel Rios. It was a memorable experience. We made the most of our time in Spain by spending extended periods on the country's beautiful summer beaches. Each trip lasted for about a month, allowing us to fully immerse ourselves in the vibrant coastal atmosphere.

On some occasions, we parked our car on the mainland and took short flights to visit stunning destinations like Las Palmas and Playa De Iglesias in Gran Canaria, where we enjoyed breathtaking beaches and exciting nightlife. Our journeys through Germany, France, and Spain only reinforced our belief that Spain was the ultimate destination for fun and unforgettable holidays.

During this phase of our lives, characterized by youth, ambition, and a focus on the future, the topic of having children never entered our conversations or thoughts. It simply wasn't a subject that came up, not among our friends or even Annie's sister, with whom she shared a close bond. The early and mid-80s passed by swiftly, filled with enjoyment, work, studies, and exploration.

Spain remained our go-to destination every summer, allowing us to discover the diverse regions of the country. We visited enchanting cities such as Barcelona, Madrid, Bilbao, Majorca, Las Palmas, Cordoba, Granada, Malaga, Murcia, Almeria, Seville, and many more. Driving throughout Europe proved to be a more comfortable experience for me as a black person compared to the encounters I had faced in the USA. Except for one incident in Amsterdam where a traffic police officer briefly questioned the authenticity of my identification cards, I had never faced any significant issues or scrutiny while travelling in Europe.

Nevertheless, our determination led us to reach out to the Swedish Embassy in The Hague. Unfortunately, our efforts were in vain as we were left stranded when attempting to find a phone booth to contact the Embassy. Driving through Spain proved to be hassle-free due to our distinct license plates, granting us priority even in congested areas. Remarkably, we encountered no police checkpoints on our journey through Germany and France, despite the heightened presence of law enforcement along their major highways during the peak summer season. To ensure both our health and budget remained intact, we diligently prepared our sandwiches and stocked up on biscuits, Swedish dry bread, and fruits to prevent any foodborne illnesses during the trip.

During our stay in Seville, the vibrant capital of Andalusia, Annie and I arrived at a modest motel on the outskirts of town around eight in the evening. Upon entering the reception area, we were met by a receptionist and a line of scantily clad young girls in the corridor. Requesting a room for the night, we were informed that a room was available on the top floor, but it came with the provision of a companion for the night. Firmly, I declined, stating that I was accompanied by my partner. As we made our way upstairs in search of the designated room, we found it after fifteen minutes. Suddenly, a soft knock echoed through the door, prompting me to open it. To my surprise, the receptionist, who appeared to be around fifty years old, stood alongside two girls, urging me to select one of them. Once again, I emphasized that I did not require their services, as I was already accompanied by my girlfriend.

Nonetheless, she persisted in her insistence that one of the girls accompany us for the night. I promptly shut the door. When my girlfriend emerged from the shower and inquired about the conversation, I explained the situation to her. This peculiar occurrence had taken place a few times before, once in Terrassa near Barcelona and another time in Murcia.

After approximately 40 minutes, there was yet another knock on the door. Opening it cautiously, I found the receptionist once again, accompanied by a girl. She inquired if I was certain that I didn't wish for a companion for the night, emphasizing that it was included in the price and completely free of charge. Firmly, I reiterated my disinterest, stating that if they persisted, we would check out and seek accommodation elsewhere.

That was the last we saw of her until the following morning around ten o'clock when we checked out. Fortunately, we never encountered any major technical or mechanical issues with our car during our travels, only experiencing minor setbacks. On one occasion, during scorching summer weather in France, I had to change a thermostat as the car began to overheat.

Thankfully, I had a spare and was able to fix it at a petrol station, and we continued our journey. Additionally, we had a punctured tyre in Valencia, which I replaced in approximately half an hour. I repaired the damaged tyre and resumed our travels. Aside from these minor challenges, our cars always performed admirably. Japanese cars are renowned for their reliability and fuel efficiency.

Upon our return from a month-long road trip in Spain, coming back home brought a sense of rejuvenation as we reconnected with friends and settled back into our familiar daily routines. On a picturesque Saturday afternoon in spring, we decided to take the underground train to the central station, located about 20 minutes away from our home.

As we boarded the train and settled in, our tranquillity was abruptly disrupted by the intrusion of two men who approached us. They began questioning Annie, remarking on her beauty and expressing disbelief that she would be in a relationship with someone like me—a Black man. Annie firmly responded, asserting that their opinions were irrelevant and accusing them of racism. Sensing the escalating tension, we both stood up, prepared to defend ourselves against their aggression.

Amidst the growing chaos, two elderly ladies intervened, positioning themselves between all parties involved. They boldly confronted the two men, unleashing a barrage of shouts and profanities directed at them. Astonishingly, the aggressors swiftly retreated, slowly returning to their seats. As we reached the next stop, they promptly exited the train. A couple of days later, I found myself at the supermarket near our home, located underground, which happened to be my preferred place to shop for groceries. As I approached the long electric escalator that descended underground, I noticed an elderly lady struggling with a sizable and weighty shopping bag. It was evident that she had already completed her shopping but was unable to carry or even push the burdened bag.

Approaching the elderly lady with genuine courtesy and concern, I politely asked if I could assist her with the heavy bag. However, she swiftly turned around, glared at me, and angrily shouted at me to go away, insisting that she didn't need my help. At that moment, I felt incredibly small, engulfed by a wave of embarrassment and shame.

I hurriedly stepped onto the escalator, quickly disappearing into the depths of the supermarket. Later that evening, I shared the incident with Annie. She was livid but also remorseful and ashamed that such unfortunate events were occurring and how ungrateful some people could be. I came to accept that human nature is complex—no matter how kind or reasonable one may be, there will always be those who hold contrasting perspectives and attitudes.

These experiences served as poignant lessons, allowing me to comprehend a regrettable aspect of Swedish society: not everyone possesses kindness and empathy. That particular incident that day taught me to mind my own business and refrain from involving myself with strangers or the unfamiliar. It made me realize that this society is different from what I was accustomed to in Gambia, where assistance and acts of kindness are often appreciated. It was a valuable lesson learned, leading me to cease offering help to strangers altogether. As time swiftly passed—days turning into weeks, weeks into months, and months into years—I realized how quickly time flies.

My girlfriend's parents resided far from Stockholm, and I found myself yearning for an older figure, akin to a Mumly presence, whom I could look up to and consider a guardian. Keeping in touch with loved ones back home was a challenging task during that time. Phone calls were a rarity due to exorbitant rates, and the absence of the Internet and social media further limited affordable communication options. Instead, we resorted to the age-old method of sending hand-written letters via airmail. However, the arrival of these letters could take several months, causing considerable gaps in staying connected.

There were occasions when I opted for registered-envelope letters, enclosing money for my Mum. The high cost of living in Stockholm's city centre left us with little disposable income, as the majority of our earnings went towards paying bills, particularly rent and electricity. Additionally, the expenses associated with owning and maintaining a car, as well as our annual holiday trips to Spain, added further strain to our budget.

At one point, I contemplated the idea of either relocating closer to my girlfriend's parents or having them sell their house and join us in Stockholm as a unified family. While I was working and pursuing part-time studies, Annie was in her final year at university. We ultimately decided that moving out of central Stockholm was a more practical choice, as the escalating yearly rent for our apartment became unsustainable.

We settled in the northern suburbs of Stockholm, a convenient location less than 20 minutes away from the city centre. I visited the county office in our desired area and obtained the necessary forms and information for securing a new apartment. Although my proficiency in the Swedish language was not yet flawless, I was able to communicate effectively, ensuring that everyone understood me.

As I approached the counter, I encountered a distinguished elderly woman who exuded an air of elegance. She had blonde hair and appeared to be around sixty years old. I explained my urgent need to find an apartment with my girlfriend and inquired about the quickest way to secure one. In response, she handed me a form to fill out and informed me that we would have to join a waiting list, which could take approximately a year before we were allocated an apartment.

I was taken aback by the lengthy timeframe and promptly expressed our desire to move out due to the exorbitant rent we were paying in the city centre. I emphasized our need for an apartment immediately. Curious about my background, she asked which country I hailed from, and I proudly responded that I was from the Gambia. To my surprise, the woman gasped audibly, her eyes widening with astonishment. She revealed that she had visited the Gambia on two separate occasions.

It was a remarkable coincidence, and I couldn't help but marvel at the smallness of the world. In a positive tone, she mentioned that she was planning another trip to the Gambia with a dentist friend from Dalarna, a county in central Sweden.

The woman introduced herself as Karin and disclosed that she was the high-ranking official in charge of the county office, temporarily covering for a colleague on a break. She kindly offered her phone number, inviting us to visit her at her home.

At that moment, I felt an instant connection, and I began referring to her as "My Swedish Mum." Little did I know that this encounter would mark the beginning of a profound bond, that lasted almost two decades. Karin became not only my guardian but also my best friend, as well as a cherished member of her own family, including her three grown-up children and their families. Karin's children were all leading successful lives in different fields.

Her youngest child was a doctor residing in the southern part of Stockholm. Another child held a prominent position as a finance director at NCC, an esteemed international construction company specializing in complex infrastructure projects. Lastly, her other child was a hotelier and proud owner of a business in Malmo, located in the south of Sweden.

Meanwhile, my love for Annie remained strong, but I began to notice a concerning pattern of increasing control in our relationship. It was emotionally draining and mentally exhausting. Despite repeatedly claiming that her actions stemmed from her love for me, I warned her that suppressing my freedom would eventually have dire consequences for our relationship.

I made it clear that there would come a point when I would say "Enough is enough" if she did not put an end to her manipulative behaviour and controlling tendencies.

On one occasion, we visited a restaurant called Skanstull in the southern part of Stockholm. Upon entering, we found ourselves seated in a lovely, secluded corner on the far right of the establishment. A friendly waitress approached our table, handed us the menu, and inquired about our drink preferences. In a light-hearted manner, I responded, prompting laughter among us.

The waitress returned with our drinks and proceeded to provide some information about the food we had ordered. However, Annie remained completely silent, displaying no interest in what the waitress was saying. Consequently, I felt compelled to engage in the conversation, offering cheerful comments. Throughout the interaction, Annie remained unnervingly quiet, fixating her gaze on one spot without uttering a word.

In an attempt to bridge the growing gap between us, I tried to initiate a conversation and lighten the mood with a joke, sensing that something was bothering Annie. After a wait of twenty minutes, our food arrived, accompanied by the customary comment, "Enjoy your meal." I graciously replied with a "Thank you."

However, as we began to prepare ourselves to eat, Annie turned away angrily. Observing tears streaming down her cheeks, I couldn't help but ask, "What's the matter?" And then it happened – she exploded: "Why don't you go with her if you love her?" Confused, I inquired, "Who?" To my astonishment, she pointed at the waitress.

Though unexpected, this accusation did not come as a surprise. Annie had developed a deep-seated suspicion towards me, expressing similar doubts even regarding her friends. She would make statements like, "Did you notice how that girl was looking at you? Why did you touch her? Why are you staring at her? She must be interested in more than friendship." These unfounded allegations became a constant source of sadness for me, as I had never harboured any intentions beyond kindness and pleasantness towards others.

Over time, the pressure mounted, leading me to avoid eye contact, conversations, or interactions with females altogether, regardless of whether they were Annie's relatives or friends.

As the weight of isolation and disconnection from female friends grew heavier, I found myself becoming more distant. One day, while riding the underground, Annie decided to purchase at a kiosk. I chose to wait outside on a nearby bench.

Suddenly, a well-dressed African woman, resembling a fashion model with her long winter boots, approached me and called out loudly, "My brother, is your name Sulayman?" Confused, I looked at her, trying to figure out who she was. She then asked, "Are you from the Gambia?" I replied, "Yes, my name is Sulayman." Introducing herself as Anna, she continued, "Didn't you come from Serre Kunda, Gambia?" Confirming that I did, she asked, "Is your Mum Auntie Fatima?"

With each affirmative response, the pieces fell into place, and I recognized who she was. We embraced each other warmly, laughing and expressing our joy. It had been years since we last saw each other, back when we were just nine or ten years old. As childhood neighbours and schoolmates, we shared fond memories.

Anna had been adopted by a Swedish family and taken to Sweden, cutting off contact with our Gambian community. Curiously, I asked, "How did you recognize me sitting here?" She explained that she recognized my voice as she passed by.

We exchanged contact information and, after a few weeks, Anna invited us to her lavish home. We brought an exotic flower as a gift. While enjoying her opulent surroundings and engaging in conversation, Annie suddenly excused herself to the bathroom. Concerned, I checked on her and found her in tears. I came in and decided to comfort her.

I approached Annie with empathy, realizing that her reaction stemmed from deep-seated insecurities and fears within our relationship. It was clear that she was feeling threatened and vulnerable, and her emotions were intensified by the events involving Anna. I sat down beside her and gently took her hand, providing a comforting presence. I began by acknowledging Annie's emotions and assuring her that her feelings were valid and important to me.

I emphasized that I loved her deeply and was committed to our relationship. I reassured her that there was no reason for her to worry about Anna or any potential threat to our bond. I explained that Anna's actions were merely friendly and that I had no romantic interest in her. I encouraged Annie to express her concerns and fears openly, emphasizing that our relationship was built on trust and open communication.

I asked her to share what specifically triggered her insecurities and why she felt threatened by the interaction with Anna. It was important for me to listen attentively and without judgment, creating a safe space for Annie to voice her thoughts and emotions. As Annie continued to cry, I remained patient and supportive. I reassured her that I was committed to addressing her concerns and finding a resolution together. I reminded her of the love and happiness we had shared and the strong foundation we had built. I encouraged her to trust in our bond and reminded her that I had chosen to be with her. In this delicate moment, I acknowledged that mere words might not be enough to alleviate Annie's fears.

I suggested that we seek professional help, such as couples' therapy, to navigate through these challenges. I assured her that seeking guidance from a neutral third party could provide us with the tools and strategies necessary to overcome our insecurities and build a healthier, more trusting relationship. Throughout the conversation, I remained patient, compassionate, and understanding. I held Annie close, offering physical comfort as she expressed her emotions. I reminded her that we were a team and that together we would find a way to address these issues and grow stronger as a couple. I even made a firm decision to sever all contact with Anna, vowing never to reach out to her again, even if she were to call and invite us over. I resolved to make excuses, claiming that we were occupied with other commitments. That was the turning point where I lost touch with Anna, my former neighbour and friend.

It's important to clarify that I never had any romantic interest in Anna; our connection was purely platonic. However, Anna's beauty and success seemed to stir up feelings of insecurity and jealousy in Annie. That particular night, I went to bed feeling a profound sadness, burdened by a sense of entrapment. I kept the problems within our relationship to myself, sharing them with no one. As a result, those around us perceived our relationship as flawless. Interacting with other women became a cautious endeavour for fear of causing Annie pain.

Witnessing Annie in tears was a heart-wrenching experience, and the realization that I needed to sacrifice something to restore her happiness left me bewildered and mentally drained. Jealousy, when it exceeds reasonable bounds, becomes detrimental to any relationship.

Every time we discussed it, the conversation followed the same pattern: she loved me deeply and feared losing me. Yet, I couldn't help but worry that her behaviour was pushing me away, slowly but surely. Even when I shared stories about my kind and supportive female teacher, Annie's immediate response was, "I hope she doesn't have feelings for you!" It was incredibly frustrating, and I eventually had to firmly ask her to stop.

Upon completing my language studies, I intended to pursue higher education at the university. However, due to overwhelming distractions and difficulty concentrating, I decided to postpone this endeavour. In the meantime, we found ourselves waiting longer than anticipated to secure a council apartment, leading us to continue bearing the burden of high bills at our current downtown residence.

While engrossed in our circle of friends, we occasionally made visits to her parents and embarked on our summer trips to Spain. Following graduation, Annie secured employment while also dedicating time to her ballet and yoga classes, political engagements, and other activities.

As Annie's jealous tendencies continued to escalate, I began contemplating whether it was time to leave the relationship rather than remain in a stifling, controlling, and dominant dynamic. One Friday evening, my cousin called me, and we engaged in a conversation in our native Gambian language, Wolof. After the call, Annie burst into tears. I inquired about the reason for her distress, and she expressed confusion over our choice to converse in Wolof instead of Swedish.

I reassured her that we had discussed nothing out of the ordinary, merely addressing family matters in Gambia and sharing anecdotes about the chilly weather here. I also mentioned how mischievous my cousin's young children were.

Over time, my frustration within the relationship grew, and I found myself feeling trapped in a confined space where I couldn't freely express my language. This became a significant issue for me, as it crossed a personal boundary. I believed that losing the freedom to speak my language whenever and wherever I desired was a clear line that had been crossed. I knew I needed to find a way out of the years-long ordeal I had been enduring.

Despite my attempts to address and resolve the relentless cycle of jealousy games, my efforts proved futile. Eventually, I reached a point where I realized there had to be an escape from this toxic relationship. One day, as I appeared visibly sad and down, Annie questioned me about my demeanour.

It was then that I mustered the courage to express my unhappiness with our relationship, emphasizing that she had not been taking my concerns seriously, and my patience was wearing thin. The erosion of my freedom felt deeply unhealthy for any relationship, and I believed that we were unable to change this dynamic. She looked at me and inquired about my proposed solution, asserting that she would never consider leaving me. After giving it some thought, I suggested the idea of living separately.

I mentioned a recent discussion where she had expressed a desire to move to the town where her parents resided. I responded by stating, "If you decide to move there, I won't be coming with you. We can see each other on weekends or every other week, considering it's just an hour away from Stockholm." Vasteras, where she attended school and still had many friends, was the town in question.

However, she insisted that my suggestion indicated I was planning to leave her for someone else, despite my promise to the contrary.

After a week of contemplation, she ultimately accepted the proposal and decided to move into her parents' house, a sizable villa.

After much discussion, we mutually agreed to live separately to work on the toxic aspects of our relationship and eventually reunite. I relocated to a place called Uplands Vasby, which was conveniently located twenty minutes from downtown Stockholm by train and fifteen minutes by car. Initially, I moved in with a friend in a spacious four-room apartment. However, I found myself driving through the back roads to Vasteras almost every weekend to spend time with Annie. As time passed, our meetings became less frequent due to work commitments and various obstacles that hindered our ability to come together on weekends. Gradually, our relationship began to lose its significance and importance for both of us.

I felt liberated by this change. It meant more independence, an end to tears and pressure, and a newfound sense of freedom. Despite the separation, we did manage to have one final summer holiday in Spain together. In the meantime, I decided to pursue part-time studies while working full-time at a job close to my new home. This newfound freedom allowed me to set personal goals and utilize my potential to the fullest.

Karin and I, whom I fondly called my Swedish Mum, grew even closer through our frequent and lengthy discussions about global affairs, societal issues, and politics. These conversations could last for hours, and it was during these moments that our connection deepened. Karin warmly introduced me to her family, and I was embraced as a new member with open arms. We celebrated special occasions together, like Christmas and various holidays, maintaining regular communication and weekend visits. As my relationship with Karin, my 'Swedish Mum,' deepened, we formed a strong, close-knit family, with Karin at its heart, earning immense respect from everyone. Karin was truly remarkable, characterized by her strength, independence, and intelligence. She believed in treating everyone equally and had a strong aversion to injustice.

Her travels had taken her far and wide, including living in Spain for a period when her children were young due to her dislike of Sweden's cold weather. During this time, I had yet to secure a council flat, but living with a Swedish friend proved to be convenient. Sharing the rent allowed me to save more money. Annie and I occasionally embarked on weekend trips to Copenhagen, exploring the city and its attractions such as the elephant gate (Carlsberg factory) and Tivoli. We also ventured to Oslo or Hamburg, seeking a change of scenery and indulging in excellent cuisine. Both of us shared a deep interest in visiting cultural landmarks, museums, and public attractions. These experiences took place during the early and mid-eighties, a time when our thirst for exploration and cultural immersion was at its peak.

After careful consideration, I decided to quit my job and pursue full-time studies in International Development, with a special focus on the UN system. However, to sustain myself financially, I began working as a taxi driver on weekends after successfully passing the necessary exams. To my surprise, I discovered that driving a taxi was quite lucrative. I received a percentage of the fare as my income, and all the tips I received from customers were mine to keep. Unfortunately, this newfound occupation marked the beginning of the end for my relationship with Annie. My weekends became fully occupied with taxi driving, leaving little room for us to spend time together.

I made excuses to visit her every other weekend, but gradually, our meetings grew more infrequent, fading away and fracturing our connection. At one point, Annie insisted on moving back in with me. However, considering the challenges we faced during our previous cohabitation, I requested that we postpone the discussion and engage in better planning at a later time. Truthfully, I was attempting to avoid the topic altogether, knowing that it would distract me from my studies. Being a young Black person driving a taxi in Stockholm opened my eyes to various realities. I encountered people from all walks of life, some of whom were kind and friendly, while others posed potential dangers. It was an enlightening experience that broadened my understanding of society and human interactions.

During one of my taxi rides, a customer I picked up from Kungsträdgården and drove to Östermalm turned out to be a dangerous individual. He pointed a gun at me and threatened to blow my head off if I didn't disappear without charging, even though the fare was only around 46 Swedish kronor, equivalent to approximately 5.5 US dollars. He made it clear that I should refrain from contacting the police or reporting the incident. At that moment, I simply thanked him and left, choosing not to escalate the situation further. Weekends were typically filled with people celebrating, partying, and opting for taxi rides instead of driving themselves. On another occasion, I had the opportunity to drive a United Nations diplomat home.

He was a polite, well-spoken, and well-dressed man with grey hair who complimented my driving skills, initiating a conversation with me. I shared with him my studies in International Development, and our discussion evolved into topics such as the United Nations system, global order, and poverty in Africa. As the journey progressed, we continued conversing outside his destination, extending the ride. To my surprise, he revealed that he believed I would eventually join and work for the UN organization upon completing my studies. The years passed, and I later discovered that this gentleman was none other than Rolf Ekeus, a prominent Swedish diplomat. In 1983, he served as a representative to the Conference on Disarmament, and in the 90s, he was well-known as the head of the UN Special Commission on Iraq.

As our conversation came to an end, he handed me a generous tip of one thousand kronor, far exceeding the cost of the fare, showing his appreciation for what he considered to be one of his most enjoyable taxi rides. Engaging in intellectually stimulating conversations with strangers who shared common interests was truly invigorating. It allowed us to delve into shared knowledge and discuss topics as if we had known each other for years. One of the joys of driving a taxi on weekends is the element of surprise, as you never know who you'll pick up next. It could be someone wonderful or potentially even a criminal. However, as a taxi driver, I have the right to refuse a customer or request partial payment before commencing the journey.

On a beautiful Saturday evening, I encountered a robust man with bags on Sveavägen, near Stockholm Central. He asked me to take him to a hotel and requested that I accompany him inside to inquire about room availability. However, I firmly responded that I had brought him to his destination, and it was his responsibility to pay and check for a room on his own. I made it clear that I would not wait for him once he had settled his payment. This led to his anger, and he insisted on remaining in the car, occupying the front seat.

I attempted to convince him in various ways, but my efforts proved futile. Eventually, I resorted to threatening to call the police. Surprisingly, he agreed and even challenged me to make the call. Feeling frustrated, I determined that he needed to vacate the car. I retrieved his bags from the trunk, approached the front seat, and opened the door.

I firmly held his arm, attempting to pull him out. However, he resisted, shifting his weight to the driver's side. In this deserted area near the hotel where I had parked, there was no sign of any other individuals, just the brightly lit hotel building and the two of us.

Despite my best efforts, the man's refusal to leave the car persisted, leaving me with limited options. Frustrated by the situation and the time we had spent, I grasped his right foot-pants at the bottom and pulled with all my strength. Slowly but surely, his body began to emerge from the vehicle. At that point, he relented and told me to leave him alone, assuring me that he would exit the taxi. However, he left without paying, disregarding his obligation to do so.

While I had the authority to accept or reject passengers, it was impossible to anticipate which individuals might cause trouble or refuse payment. Some even resorted to racial intimidation, but I chose to ignore such remarks and conversations.

On another occasion, I picked up three individuals from Stockholm Centre, destined for a place called Farsta, approximately a twenty-minute journey. As we neared our destination, one of them casually mentioned that he had no money to pay for the trip and asked if the others did. I immediately inquired, "Who will be responsible for the fare?" In response, the others admitted to having spent all their money at the bar, leaving me certain that they had no intention of paying. Glancing at the rearview mirror, I observed them laughing and engaging in unrelated conversations. I intervened once again, asking them explicitly who would be responsible for settling the fare.

As the three passengers vehemently denied any responsibility for payment, I activated the electric locks, secured all the doors, and drove directly to the nearest police station. Throughout the journey, they continued to protest, exclaiming, "Are you taking us to the police station just because we have no money?" Upon arrival, I swiftly exited the taxi and locked the vehicle from the outside, relying on its advanced security systems. Inside the police station, I explained the situation to a female police officer, who accompanied me outside. She requested that I unlock the car, and reluctantly, I complied. The officer proceeded to gather their personal information, which was duly recorded and then requested that they pay the fare amounting to eighty kronor. However, as they reached into their wallets, it became apparent that they were devoid of any funds.

Frustrated and seething with anger, I left the scene without uttering a word, fully aware that my efforts were in vain and that I would not be compensated. I never learned what became of them, but I assumed that the police eventually released them. Driving a taxi in Stockholm, particularly as a Black man, necessitated a considerable amount of tolerance. Some customers would immediately engage in provocation, making nonsensical comments or posing irrelevant questions. Despite my Taxi ID card being visibly displayed on the dashboard, some individuals insisted on verifying my identity, even though the photograph depicted me. Many times, I reached a point of frustration and simply asked such individuals to exit the vehicle. On one occasion, I picked up a passenger who was headed to Huddinge in the southern part of Stockholm. Throughout the trip, he engaged in a monologue, talking to himself. Upon arriving at his destination, he unexpectedly began to weep. Curious, I inquired, "What is wrong?"

He replied, "I'm about to graduate as a doctor next week, but my girlfriend has left me." He opened up about their relationship and the difficulties they had encountered. I listened attentively, provided empathy, and offered guidance to help him find the strength to move forward with his new life as a doctor.

It was a compassionate and empathetic decision to take the time to listen and offer advice to the passenger who was going through a difficult time. Sometimes, providing a listening ear and offering a different perspective can make a positive impact on someone's well-being. In a society where communication is often limited, people may seize the opportunity during a taxi ride to engage in meaningful conversations, seeking connection and understanding. It is important to approach these interactions with maturity, kindness, and assertiveness, while also being mindful of personal safety and boundaries.

As a taxi driver, it becomes apparent that the job extends beyond simply driving passengers from one location to another. It involves providing a supportive presence and, at times, assuming a counselling role.

People may discuss a wide range of topics, from politics and social issues to personal matters concerning their families and private lives. This highlights the fundamental human need for connection and communication, even with strangers. It underscores the significance of social interaction for our mental and emotional well-being. While balancing the responsibilities of driving and studying, I continued to navigate the taxi industry, offering valuable service to customers while pursuing my educational goals. This period likely provided me with diverse experiences and perspectives, further enriching my understanding of people and the world around me.

Chapter 3

Life In Sudan

I was presented with an opportunity to work in Sudan by an American friend who is an epidemiologist. This job is part of a new project established in collaboration with USAID and the Ministry of Health of Sudan.

Considering my interest in poverty and African development, along with the chance to explore unseen parts of the continent, I believed accepting the offer was the right decision.

Upon receiving the offer, several questions arose in my mind. Could I adapt to living in a country with Sharia laws and endure the extreme heat? These were just a couple of the challenges that crossed my mind. Transitioning directly from Scandinavia to the scorching desert was not an easy adjustment.

However, I viewed this opportunity as an exciting adventure, especially since I had the support and trust of someone I knew. Thus, I decided to embrace the role of an administrator and put my studies on hold until further notice. This all occurred when I was in my early twenties.

I opted to travel with Ethiopian Airlines, which I highly recommend as one of the world's top airlines. The journey took me to Addis Ababa, where I had an overnight layover before reaching Khartoum the next day around midday.

Stepping out of the plane, I was hit by the intense heat for the first time, an experience that will forever be etched in my memory. I was so taken aback that I almost considered going back onto the plane. However, observing other passengers calmly descending the stairs, I followed suit and met my friend, who couldn't help but laugh at my reaction.

We swiftly left the airport premises and got into a comfortably air-conditioned Ford Ranger, heading straight to the office. Even the office had a cooling air-conditioning system in place.

During my initial weeks in Sudan, I faced some inconveniences. It was challenging to fully concentrate due to constant sweating and a general feeling of unease. However, I reminded myself that I had the option to leave the job if I found the conditions unbearable.

The most difficult aspect was undoubtedly the scorching heat and the long daylight hours. The sun would already be blazing by around 8 a.m. and wouldn't set until approximately 7 p.m.

This level of heat was unlike anything I had experienced even in the Gambia, where temperatures could also reach high levels, especially during summertime, going up to forty degrees Celsius or more. Sudan presented a completely different environment from what I was accustomed to in the Gambia. The food in Sudan was a delightful exploration of flavours and aromas. From aromatic stews and grilled meats to freshly baked bread and vibrant spices, every meal was a culinary adventure. The locals took pride in their traditional dishes, and I savoured every bite. However, it was the ubiquitous presence of tea that truly fascinated me. Wherever I went, I was always served tea in medium-sized transparent drinking glasses, generously sweetened with sugar. Beyond the gastronomic delights, the people of Sudan left an indelible impression on me. They were incredibly kind and friendly, always welcoming me with warm smiles and genuine hospitality.

As I settled into my new surroundings, I was introduced to an American Club, a haven that provided a sense of familiarity. Within its premises, I had access to amenities such as a swimming pool, an excellent restaurant, a tennis court, and a film club. It was here that I made new friends who became my companions throughout my stay. Our work took us beyond the comforts of the city as we embarked on field trips to refugee camps located outside of Khartoum. These experiences allowed us to witness firsthand the challenging conditions faced by the displaced population and enabled us to evaluate projects and provide comprehensive reports and recommendations to the Sudanese government. Simultaneously, I found myself settling into an office near the University, working closely with the Ministry of Health.

The ministry office was often abuzz with activity, with occasional protests adding to the clamour. Managing the organization's vehicles and assets, placing orders for office supplies, and keeping track of fuel and office expenses became part of my administrative responsibilities. Amidst the bustling routine, the Acropolis Hotel in downtown Khartoum emerged as a favoured meeting spot for expatriates, myself included. Originally established by a Greek family who relocated to Khartoum after World War II, the hotel offered a welcoming atmosphere, delicious food, and a clean environment. The rooftop seating area provided a refreshing breeze and the perfect setting for engaging conversations and discussions. Overall, my time in Sudan was a remarkable journey of discovery. The distinctiveness of the food, language, culture, and traditional beliefs intertwined with the warmth and generosity of the Sudanese people left an enduring impression on me. After spending three months in Khartoum, an affiliated office was established in El-Obeid, the capital of Kurdufan.

This expansion brought additional administrative tasks and the responsibility of managing a guest house to my plate. The journey from Khartoum to El-Obeid, spanning over four hundred kilometres, was not an easy one. The lack of paved or identifiable roads meant that our travel through the desert relied heavily on a compass, and the trip could often stretch to fourteen hours or more. These challenges were exacerbated during sandstorms, which could rage on for days before subsiding and allowing the dust to settle. Upon settling into a large villa in El-Obeid, I discovered that my closest neighbour was the British Council, led by a Sudanese individual named Ahmed. To ensure uninterrupted operation, even during frequent power outages, I decided to extend a cable over the fence, providing them with access to electricity from our 28 KVA standby generator.

Some colleagues suggested that I should charge the British Council for this service, but considering the Council's limited budget and the benefit it brought to the local community, particularly their library services, I never requested any compensation. Adjacent to the British Council, there was a tennis court that soon became my favourite spot for spending Saturday or Sunday mornings playing tennis. Having settled in El-Obeid, my primary focus shifted to managing the office and conducting occasional trips to Khartoum for consultations. It was crucial to ensure that we always had an adequate supply of office materials and sufficient fuel for our fleet of vehicles, which consisted of four Ford Rangers and a Land Rover. Managing the transportation needs became a significant part of our budgetary considerations. The dynamic between Khartoum and El-Obeid created a balance between administrative responsibilities and the occasional need for consultations and supplies.

Despite the challenges and distances involved, I adapted to the demands of the role, constantly striving to ensure the smooth operation of our office and the provision of services to the local community. Running the guest house, managing wages, rent, and various miscellaneous tasks were among the responsibilities entrusted to me. Our work often involved embarking on field trips, sometimes venturing into regions like Darfur and Kurdufan to conduct studies on nomadic communities. This endeavour was not without its challenges, as reaching and engaging with these communities required perseverance and resourcefulness. In El-Obeid, there were days when I would wake up early, around six or seven, before the scorching sun made its presence felt. I would embark on a jog to the nearby airport, a couple of kilometres away from my house. Collaborating with esteemed organizations such as UNICEF, UNHCR, and other multilateral entities, our team worked tirelessly to exchange and compare data, ideas, and reports.

Our collective aim was to address prevalent issues such as diseases, malnutrition, and female genital mutilation (FGM), which inflicted significant harm on women, particularly in refugee camps. Working alongside a dedicated team of doctors, we made critical decisions, crafted reports, and implemented programmes to achieve set objectives that would have a tangible impact on people's lives. It was an immense challenge, but also an undertaking of great significance and a lifelong learning experience. Reflecting on those experiences now, considering the overwhelming poverty and destitution we encountered and the demanding circumstances we operated in, I feel a sense of pride in having contributed to such noble work for the betterment of humanity. The passion to continue making a difference in that part of the world still burns within me, as people continue to endure suffering today.

During my two-year stay in El-Obeid, I formed a close-knit circle of friends, both expatriates and Sudanese locals. Among my expatriate friends were the UNICEF representative, an American couple working for CARE, an Indian-American professor and his wife (who used to invite me with hot delicious Indian dishes) associated with USAID, as well as another American guy who was attached to the professor, representing one of the top universities in the United States. Additionally, I developed strong bonds with many Sudanese friends, particularly the doctors I collaborated with. Interestingly, the locals became more intrigued by my presence after learning that I was a Muslim.

Being aware of my religion led to numerous invitations to their homes for Friday lunches or dinners. As I visited various Sudanese households and shared meals with them, I observed that the women or wives were always absent from sight. Everything seemed to be pre-arranged before my arrival or handled by the male members of the household during my visits. However, within the office environment, I had the opportunity to work closely with women. My secretary was an Egyptian lady proficient in English, and another local administrative staff member collaborated with several female doctors from the Ministry of Health.

Eventually, my contract came to an end, and I departed for Sweden. However, the experiences and conditions I witnessed in refugee camps in Sudan continued to haunt me for months. The misery and hardships endured by the people I encountered left a lasting impact. I have always felt the urge to do more for the extremely impoverished in Africa. The staggering disparity between the wealthy and impoverished nations is vast and inherently unjust, fueling my determination to contribute further to addressing these issues.

After deciding to connect with the UN organization in Stockholm, which served as the coordinating body for all UN agencies in Sweden, I recognized the need to settle down first. Soon enough, I managed to secure a council flat, purchased a car, and began working for a small company involved in the manufacturing of inhalators. During this time, I avoided contacting Annie, fearing that she might want to reconcile and move in with me. I developed a good friendship with the company owner where I worked, who also served as the CEO. He and I would engage in conversations about politics and global affairs whenever he visited the office, much to the displeasure of my immediate boss.

Our camaraderie extended beyond work-related discussions, as we started playing tennis together every Tuesday afternoon as part of an employee welfare programme initiated by the company. All employees were permitted to book tennis time even during working hours. Gradually, our shared interests led us to venture into golf, spending hours together on Saturdays. However, my close rapport with the company owner seemed to unsettle my line manager. One afternoon, he called me into his office, his expression a mix of anger and bewilderment. I took a seat opposite him, uncertain about the reason for his demeanour. Without hesitation, he confronted me with a blush on his face, saying, "I know the game you're playing, and I don't like it." Surprised, I inquired about his meaning. He continued, revealing his concerns, "I know you want to take my position, but I will not allow it!"

The confrontation caught me off guard, as I had never harboured any ambitions to usurp his role. However, it became evident that my burgeoning friendship with the company owner had ignited these suspicions in my manager. I reassured him of my intentions, expressing my commitment to my current position and the desire to contribute positively to the company. Despite the tension at that moment, I aimed to mend the strained relationship and foster a more harmonious work environment moving forward. I was taken aback by my line manager's accusation and questioned why he believed I had any intention of undermining his position. He expressed his concerns, stating that he saw my relationship with the company owner heading in a direction he disapproved of. I reassured him that my friendship with the top boss had no connection to him or our work.

I made it clear that our friendship revolved solely around shared values, and interests in global affairs, politics, economics, the stock market, and sports like tennis and golf. I emphasized that our conversations never touched upon him or any work-related matters. I also explicitly conveyed that I had no desire to assume his position and that I was content with my current role, his leadership, and his position within the company. Having addressed the issue, I left his office, and the topic was never brought up again. Despite this incident, my friendship and relationship with the company owner continued to flourish. I chose not to disclose what had transpired with my line manager, as it seemed unrelated to my interactions with him. Meanwhile, the atmosphere with my line manager became increasingly uneasy and difficult.

He began ignoring me altogether, leaving others to speculate on the reasons behind his behaviour. Some believed he was fearful of my presence, while others thought he had a fondness for me and chose to remain silent, allowing me freedom in my work. However, I recognized that these dynamics were simply manifestations of office politics and chose not to take them too seriously. I remained focused on my job and continued to maintain a professional demeanour, disregarding the tension surrounding the situation. It was important for me to rise above office politics and maintain a positive attitude, focusing on my responsibilities and contributing to the company to the best of my abilities. A few months after the tense meeting with my line manager, the company owner decided to embark on a long holiday in Texas, USA.

However, just three days after his departure, something unimaginable occurred—I received a dismissal letter from my line manager. Fortunately, in Sweden, employment termination requires substantial grounds, including the issuance of two warning letters before resorting to any dismissal. Recognizing this, I immediately reached out to the Union for advice and assistance. It was confirmed that my termination lacked valid justification. The Union representative visited the workplace, and we entered into a preliminary negotiation phase with the company. When pressed for the reason behind my dismissal, my line manager evaded the question, simply stating that I "must leave and must leave now," emphasizing their willingness to provide compensation. It became evident that my presence was unwanted, and my manager was adamant about my departure. As I had a month's notice period, there was ample time for negotiations regarding the terms and conditions of my departure, particularly the compensation package.

Remarkably, the negotiations spanned almost two weeks before reaching an agreement on a generous compensation offer, ultimately leading to my departure from the company. On the following Friday, I began working full-time at a position closer to my home, where I had previously been employed part-time. Reflecting on the circumstances surrounding my termination, I couldn't help but perceive my manager's actions as a result of his lack of confidence, insecurity, and inferiority complex, which ultimately made him appear vulnerable in the workplace. Despite the unfortunate event that transpired, I chose to focus on the positive outcome of the negotiations and the new opportunity that awaited me in my new workplace. It was a fresh start, allowing me to leave behind the negative environment and embark on a new chapter.

Upon my friend's return from his holiday, he reached out to me to inquire about the situation that unfolded during his absence. Initially, I tried to downplay the matter and avoid providing a detailed explanation. However, during a golf game we shared, he expressed his apology but was also curious about what happened. I provided a brief overview of what had occurred, refraining from criticizing or speaking ill of my former boss. He insisted that I return to the company. I informed him that I had already begun a new job and expressed my satisfaction with the compensation I had received. Within a month, I received news that the line manager who had previously terminated my employment had also been sacked. Amid these developments, my amicable relationship with the owner continued. During one conversation, he mentioned that the office was facing issues with the current state of cleaning and asked if I knew of a good cleaning company. I replied honestly, stating that I had no knowledge or connections in that field.

The owner then proposed a brilliant idea—he suggested that I register and start my own cleaning company, offering me a contract to clean the office. I was immediately captivated by the opportunity. Excitedly, I later shared the proposal with Karin, who also saw it as a fantastic venture. Given her recent retirement, she assured me that she would assist with the necessary paperwork, as she had more free time during the day. This would be my first experience as a CEO, and I decided to register the company as 'Solomon's All Cleaning AB'. I procured all the required materials, including a polishing machine, and secured a one-year contract to clean both the production area and the offices during evening hours. Embarking on this new entrepreneurial journey filled me with anticipation and motivation. I was grateful for the offer, support and opportunity to establish my own business with an immediate contract. With Karin's assistance and the necessary resources in place, I was ready to provide high-quality cleaning services and ensure the office maintained a pristine environment.

With my full-time job and the newly established cleaning company, I hired five part-time cleaners, appointing Eva as the supervisor to ensure efficient and coordinated work. The cleaning operations were scheduled for two hours a day, Monday to Friday. To maintain a high standard of work, I made it a practice to visit the office every Friday evening, assess the cleanliness, interact with former colleagues, and take note of any specific requirements or requests.

On one Saturday night, around midnight, I decided to visit a club near my previous residence in the town centre of Stockholm. It was a lively venue with a dance floor, a small bar, and a restaurant. As I entered the club, I made my way to the dance floor and noticed a tall blonde girl in the corner.

Intrigued, I approached her and struck up a conversation. We later decided to grab a bite to eat, and gradually, she became my girlfriend.

When the night was over, I offered to drive her home. To my surprise, she directed me to an area known as Centralen, which is the heart of Stockholm. She pointed out a building where she lived and mentioned that it was not just offices, but also residential units. Curious, I asked how she managed to secure such a place. She revealed that her Dad had purchased the three-room flat for her, and it happened to be located beneath the headquarters of Sweden's largest bank, Nord Banken. It was an unexpected revelation, but it added an intriguing aspect to our budding relationship.

I listened attentively as Eli shared her story, acknowledging that her Dad's disapproval of her modelling career and her relationship with a Black man had caused a deep rift in their relationship. A few days after I met with Eli, I received an anxious phone call one afternoon. She had confided in her father about our relationship. The intensity of the situation was evident from her tearful phone call to me during her dispute with her Dad.

After she left work and returned home, she called me again, still upset and crying. I offered her my support and understanding, comforting her during this challenging time. Later, once I finished work, she came over to my place, filled with anger towards her Dad and expressing her frustration at his racist remarks.

Eli's fame and recognition in Stockholm were apparent wherever we went. We often enjoyed the perks of her popularity, receiving complimentary meals at different restaurants, with the staff recognizing and accommodating her. Through Eli, I had the opportunity to meet members of a world-famous pop group who had grown up in the same area as me.

They formed the band there and went on to achieve international success, with their songs topping charts worldwide. Their presence on TV and radio stations added an exciting element to our experiences together, creating moments of joy and laughter.

They shared their childhood anecdotes with me, recounting their struggles and the formation of their band. Particularly memorable were the times when they would play loud music, causing disturbances in the neighbourhood and receiving repeated warnings from the police. However, all their efforts paid off when they secured their first record deals and embarked on world tours. During my time with them, I also had the opportunity to meet a renowned artist who had achieved global fame in the 1990s with their band. This artist happened to be a close friend of Eli's.

Additionally, I visited the home of another famous Swedish artist and songwriter, known for their chart-topping hits, especially in the UK. Remarkably, they maintained their friendship over the years. This artist, known for their abstract and spiritual poetry, possessed a humble and modest demeanour. He often used to say, "Salomon, you are a good person; I can see it in your face."

Accompanied by Eli, I never experienced any difficulty gaining entry to restaurants or clubs in Stockholm. Every time we approached the entrance, she would hold my hand and confidently declare to the doormen, "It's me and my boyfriend, Salomon," allowing us to pass through without a second glance. We shared many enjoyable moments. After a few months, I decided to take a two-week vacation and travelled to Virginia, USA. It turned out to be a delightful trip, during which I had the opportunity to visit renowned attractions such as the Smithsonian Museum, climb the Washington Monument, explore the Pentagon and Capitol Hill, tour the White House, and immerse myself in the National Air and Space Museum, among others.

Upon my return from my holiday, I drove straight to her place, and our joy at seeing each other was evident. I handed her a souvenir I had brought from the USA, and she suggested that we have dinner at a nearby restaurant owned by one of her friends, if there was room available. We entered the restaurant, found a table, perused the menu, and ordered our meals along with some refreshing lime water. The food was delicious, and the ambience was delightful. As we finished our meal, we sat there, engaged in gentle conversation, looking into each other's eyes, and holding hands across the table.

Then, out of the blue, she said, "I need to tell you something." I responded, "What is it? Is it about your Dad again?" She shook her head and said, "No, it's not about that. We haven't spoken since our argument. It's something else, and I don't know how to say it." Curious, I encouraged her, saying, "Please, go ahead. I'm eager to know."

However, she hesitated for the next fifteen minutes, her tears gradually streaming down her cheeks. I urged her to share whatever was on her mind. Eventually, she gathered the courage to speak, saying, "You know how much I love you, but I have done something wrong." I inquired, "Wrong? What do you mean?" She continued, "When you were away, my ex-boyfriend, the model from New York whom I mentioned to you before, came to visit for a week. We met, and we ended up being intimate. I'm so sorry!" She kept repeating her apologies: "I'm sorry, I'm sorry!" I reassured her, saying, "It's alright. I appreciate your honesty and respect for telling me, even though it could have remained a secret."

Suddenly, her demeanour changed, and she seemed like a small child in my hands, desperately seeking forgiveness. Although I felt disappointed and let down, I made every effort to remain composed and conceal any signs of grievance or disappointment. I reassured her, calming her down, and said, "You have apologized, and I wholeheartedly forgive you." Soon after, we decided to walk back to her place since I had parked my car on a nearby street. As we reached her place, she held the glass-stainless steel electronic door open for me, and I mentioned, "You know, I told you I'm exhausted and have to wake up early for work tomorrow. I have a lot to catch up on after being away for two weeks." She responded, "Oh, so you're not staying the night?" I replied, "Not tonight, but perhaps over the weekend. And no, I'm not mad at you," with a wink.

We spent another hour there, standing together as she continued to apologize, blame herself, and express her remorse. We hugged and kissed, but eventually, I left and headed home, feeling disappointed and uncomfortable. She called me late that night, but I cut the conversation short as I grew tired of hearing her endless regrets, self-blame, and apologies. The next day, she called again, but I chose not to answer the phone. As she failed to reach me for some time, she left a message acknowledging that she understood I was upset about what had transpired.

After two days of avoiding communication with her, I returned home one evening after going for a run, only to find her sitting outside my place. She was once again in tears, apologizing for what had happened and expressing her belief that I had forgiven her. I made it clear that I wasn't angry with her but insisted that before we could move forward, she needed to undergo an AIDS test.

At that time, AIDS was a highly discussed and concerning topic, particularly in Sweden and the Western world. Engaging in risky behaviour was something to be cautious about. AIDS being an incurable disease, witnessing people getting infected and losing their lives should have served as a wake-up call for everyone to be careful. She responded, "Yes, I will take the AIDS test tomorrow." I realized that our relationship would never be the same again. The fundamental pillars of any relationship, trust and confidence, had already been shattered.

We spent hours talking on the phone afterwards, but I gradually withdrew my emotional attachment to her. I refused to retrieve my clothes and shoes from her place. Instead, I focused on my daily activities, keeping myself occupied with Karin, the rest of my family, and other matters that helped divert my attention from her. After a short period, a couple from Marsta, a town approximately fifteen minutes away from my place, invited me for dinner on a Sunday. Unbeknownst to me, other people were also present at the gathering. Consequently, I brought a cake dessert and a couple of soft drinks with me.

I attended the dinner as planned. The gentleman's partner was a pleasant English lady who had recently relocated to Sweden and was in the process of learning the Swedish language. It was during this gathering that I had the opportunity to meet a stunning Russian girl, who introduced herself as a fellow language learner in the same class as the English lady, who would eventually become my wife for the next five years. We all enjoyed a delightful dinner together, engaging in conversation and exchanging telephone numbers. A week later, she visited me, and we spent time getting to know each other better. I discovered that she had previously worked as a photographic model in Russia before moving to Sweden six years ago. It was evident that I had always possessed an appreciation for beauty in women.

I had a keen eye for qualities such as intelligence, ambition, love, care, and style. My wife, whom I'll refer to as Sana, embodied all these attributes. She was not only beautiful but also intelligent and charming. Our relationship flourished, leading us to get married, and she moved in with me. We had a civil ceremony, attended by Karin, our entire family, a few close friends, and co-workers.

The occasion was celebrated with abundant food and joy. Sana, much like myself, regarded Karin as her Mum figure. We spent a significant amount of time at Karin's place since we lived only three minutes away. Sana worked at Arlanda, the main airport, which was approximately a fifteen-minute commute from our home.

On a Saturday afternoon, we opted to have lunch at a Japanese restaurant situated in a bustling mall at the heart of the town. As we made our way through the entrance, a group of people caught our attention—it turned out to be a fashion agent actively scouting for beautiful girls. We grabbed a few flyers and informational materials they were distributing before proceeding to enjoy our meal at the restaurant. Later, back at home, Sana took a closer look at the flyers and felt a surge of inspiration to pursue a career as a photo model. She diligently submitted her photos and filled out a comprehensive form, providing details about her height, body type, eye colour, hair colour, and other pertinent information. Fortunately, she also had photographs from her prior work in Russia, including catalogues.

Two weeks elapsed, and an invitation arrived for Sana to visit the modelling agency. After spending a few hours in town, she called me excitedly to share the news—she had been offered a contract as a catalogue model. While catalogue models primarily work in commercial settings, promoting items like bras, underwear, women's clothing, hats, earrings, and more, where strict height requirements are not paramount, Sana celebrated the opportunity with great enthusiasm. To mark the occasion, we gathered with some friends, including Karin, who prepared a scrumptious salad and an apple pie dessert. Sana decided to leave her job at the airport and wholeheartedly dedicate herself to her burgeoning modelling career. During that summer, we embarked on a two-week holiday in Moscow. Regrettably, we found that the culinary experiences in Moscow did not meet our expectations, regardless of where we dined. Nonetheless, the city itself appeared remarkably well-organized, with diligent individuals taking care of its wide streets through constant cleaning efforts.

During our visit to Moscow, we immersed ourselves in its rich history and cultural landmarks. We explored the iconic Kremlin, marvelling at its grandeur, and embarked on a fascinating walking tour that took us to the vast Cathedral and the State Duma. Moscow University also captivated us, as we wandered through its different faculties, appreciating the pursuit of knowledge taking place within its walls. To appreciate the city from a different perspective, we embarked on a Moscow River Boat tour, allowing us to witness the city's beauty from the water. Additionally, we visited the Patriotic War Museum of 1812, delving into Russia's legendary past.

In late June month, a familiar sight greeted us—the ground covered in poplar fluff, which also adorned rooftops throughout the city. As I continued living a well-organized life, surrounded by great friends and pursuing my interests such as reading, running, playing golf, and enjoying occasional dinners, I maintained a strong commitment to planning, organization, and follow-through.

Honouring my word, particularly with appointments and agreements with friends, became a foundational aspect of building my reputation as a reliable and trustworthy individual. However, despite my focus on the present, my mind often drifted back to my experiences in Sudan and the profound impact they had on me. Through my network of contacts, I became acquainted with a kindred spirit named Inga, a headmistress nearing retirement age at a high school. We formed a close friendship, and I found myself naturally gravitating towards relationships with individuals older than myself. Inga's husband, a professor at Stockholm University, became another fascinating conversational partner, engaging in lengthy discussions about global affairs without ever tiring. Additionally, Inga's involvement in an orphanage project in Ghana, where her school exposed children to different cultures and experiences, further deepened our connection.

The orphanage project that Inga initiated was a charitable endeavour aimed at facilitating a cultural exchange between children from different backgrounds. As Inga approached retirement, there was no one within the school willing to take on the immense responsibilities associated with the project. In our discussions, I agreed to step forward and register as a non-governmental organization (NGO) to continue and expand the project. Initially, the project involved fewer than sixty children, but I aspired to broaden its scope by establishing a primary school within the orphanage premises. This expansion would allow the children to seamlessly transition from kindergarten to primary school without having to leave the orphanage or remain idle within its compound. The idea garnered widespread support, and I embarked on a mission to recruit new members and volunteers to support and further develop the project.

I placed advertisements in local newspapers, seeking individuals interested in joining and contributing to the cause. The response exceeded my expectations, with over thirty people expressing their interest in becoming members within the following week. Thus, the Vasby UN organization officially became an NGO, collaborating with other UN organizations in Stockholm and Sollentuna. In Swedish, the organization was formally known as Vasby FN Förening, solidifying its presence and impact within the community. The project had evolved into a successful initiative, attracting support from both elderly individuals and young enthusiasts, all eager to learn more and contribute to the cause.

Over two years, the organization experienced remarkable growth, expanding its membership to over a hundred individuals. I assumed the position of Chairman and continued to be re-elected at the annual general meetings (AGMs) for several years. Our ambitions led us to further expand the orphanage, accommodating seven hundred and fifty children and establishing a primary school comprising fifteen classroom blocks. In quiet moments, I often contemplated the plight of those less fortunate children, recognizing that education held the key to offering them a brighter and more fulfilling future. The organization operated through various small committees, with members taking on specific tasks and responsibilities in their areas of interest. I wanted to ensure that everyone had a sense of ownership and actively participated in the organization's endeavours. We encouraged members to take pride in their contributions, as they played a pivotal role in instilling hope in the lives of these underprivileged children.

Collaboration with Stockholm UN Org allowed us to organize and attend numerous conferences, seminars, and workshops, all aimed at furthering our cause. Juggling my responsibilities as the Chairman, running a cleaning company as a full-time job, and finding time for golf, I found it challenging to squeeze in any extra commitments. However, I always made it a priority to spend quality time with my wife, Sana. While I was not personally interested in attending fashion shows, Sana had the opportunity to travel to Paris, Milan, and London with friends, thanks to invitations from her agent. On one occasion, Sana's agent organized a Christmas dinner at one of Stockholm's popular restaurants, where over fifty guests, including myself, gathered to celebrate the festive season.

Anticipation filled the air as we eagerly awaited a magnificent feast. The tables were adorned with delectable dishes, and our guests began to arrive at the entrance. Arriving promptly before nine in the evening, my wife, Sana, and I approached the door. While Sana was warmly welcomed and granted entry, I encountered a different fate. The lady at the door uttered apologetically, "I'm sorry, but you cannot come in." Responding swiftly, I explained, "I am here with my wife, and she was invited by her agent." Curious, the lady at the door engaged in a conversation with a gentleman stationed nearby. In a matter of seconds, Sana returned, confused about the unfolding situation as she assumed I was right behind her.

Firmly holding their ground, the door attendants insisted that I would not be allowed inside. Sana's anger boiled, and she sought out her agent for assistance. Inside the venue, over thirty guests had already settled in, engaging in conversations over soft drinks. Upon learning of the predicament, my wife's agents grew infuriated. They promptly contacted the restaurant owner, informing him that the entire party would be leaving. It later became apparent to me that hiring the restaurant until midnight, along with food and drinks, was a costly affair. Chaos ensued at the door, as other guests stepped forward to voice their anger and disappointment regarding the injustice and racial discrimination displayed. Some suggested we abandon the place and vow never to return. Unanimously, the sentiment echoed, "Let's all depart." Thus, we exited the restaurant and decided to seek an alternative destination.

Despite their regrets, the two doorkeepers made earnest efforts to rectify the situation and persuade us to return to the restaurant. They engaged in phone conversations with the restaurant owner, attempting to convince us to reconsider. In the meantime, one of our group members reached out to a friend who owned a restaurant within walking distance. Fortunately, we were warmly received at the alternative venue and spent the remainder of the evening there, until approximately three in the morning. The following morning, Sana remained deeply upset about what had transpired. She shared the unfortunate incident with Karin, who also expressed strong emotions and insisted on pursuing legal action against the restaurant owner and the guards. Karin believed that a civil case should be brought forth as discrimination is illegal in Sweden.

However, I found it difficult to entertain the idea seriously, knowing that the police and courts in Sweden often fail to address discrimination cases adequately, particularly those involving Black individuals. The anti-discrimination laws in the country possess numerous loopholes, rendering them ineffective in protecting minorities from discrimination and racism. I didn't harbour as much anger as Sana or Karin because I had experienced previous instances of being denied entry to restaurants or clubs. I had learned to swallow the bitter pill and move on. However, someone who held a significant place in my psyche, emotional well-being, and dreams was my late Mum, who passed away after I left the Gambia. Many nights, I would sit alone and shed tears for her. In my dreams, she often appeared as if she were still alive, a constant presence in my thoughts and emotions.

The values of discipline, organizational skills, and other qualities that I possess are all a testament to the way my Mum raised me during my childhood, for which I am profoundly grateful. Her loss was an unimaginable and surreal experience, unlike anything I had ever encountered. Both Sana and Karin held immense respect for my Mum, as I often spoke of her with admiration and fondness. The emotional bond between us was incredibly strong, and no one else in the world cared for and protected me the way she did. My Mum was an exceptional woman, and I cherished her deeply.

After her passing, I was filled with anger, disappointment, and frustration, leading me to make a solemn vow never to return to the Gambia again. Losing her meant losing everything and feeling that there was nothing left for me there. Although my Dad was still alive, advancing in age, our relationship was never the same as the one I had with my Mum. She was my everything, my guiding light in life. However, I received news one day that my Dad had fallen ill. I promptly sent him money and even purchased a car from Germany, which I arranged to be shipped to him. I believed that it would be a valuable asset for him to hire a driver and utilize the vehicle as a taxi for his livelihood. Meanwhile, I kept myself occupied with various activities, but deep down, I always had the idea of restarting and completing my studies at Linkoping University, where I had left off, lingering in the back of my mind.

Amidst my busy schedule, I realized that to pursue my ambitions, I would have to make sacrifices. International Development has always been a subject of immense interest to me. However, after numerous conversations with Sana about the possibility of resuming my studies, I decided to temporarily set aside the idea of changing our lifestyle to prioritize education. As the chairman of an NGO for the past few years and managing my cleaning company with a team of five employees, I found myself drawn to the field of Management and Leadership. This newfound interest prompted me to conduct thorough research on the subject, leading me to believe it was the right path for me.

To deepen my understanding, I purchased excellent introductory management books by Peter Drucker, renowned as the Dad of Management, from 'Akademibokhandeln'. Now, all that remained was finding quiet time to dedicate to my studies. The more I delved into the realm of Management and Leadership, the more my interest grew. Over time, I expanded my self-learning to include influential figures such as Prahalad, Gary Hamel, and Michael Porter. Tom Peters' book 'In Search of Excellence' became one of my favourites, alongside Mark McCormack's 'What They Don't Teach You at Harvard Business School'. Subjects like Management, Marketing, Finance, and Leadership captivated my attention as I aspired to become a great leader someday. Self-teaching demanded discipline and unwavering dedication, but the rewards were worth the effort.

Management remained my primary focus, and I actively applied what I learned in various aspects of my life. Business Management became a valuable tool as I served as a practising leader in both my roles, as chairman of the NGO and as the Director of my cleaning company. During this time, I discovered a self-development and motivational speaker named Tony Robbins. His teachings gained immense popularity and became a prerequisite for anyone aspiring to personal growth and leadership. I invested in his cassette audio package titled 'Personal Power', which proved to be a valuable resource for self-development and goal setting.

Motivated by my progress, I decided to further my education and enrolled in a distance learning course on Business Management and Leadership at Cambridge Tutorial College. Eventually, I completed the programme and earned an Advanced Diploma. Given the busy nature of my life and my deep love for my wife, Sana, starting a family had not been a priority for us. Although Sana had jokingly mentioned having children once, the topic did not resurface in our conversations. On the other hand, Karin expressed how beautiful it would be to see a child from Sana and me. However, I made it clear that we had no plans for children at the moment, as our lives were already filled with numerous commitments and responsibilities.

Despite my longing to go for long daytime jogs, time constraints limited me to quick runs around my residence in the late evenings. These brief jogs, lasting about twenty to thirty minutes, were better than nothing. As time passed, I made an effort to incorporate running into my routine, aiming for three to four sessions per week. I participated in a couple of local runs, including half-marathons, before setting my sights on the ultimate challenge: the Stockholm Marathon. Upon completing my first marathon, I received a certificate, and a medal, and even had my name published in Dagens Nyheter, Sweden's largest newspaper. It was a proud achievement for me, and from that point forward, I decided to participate in the Stockholm Marathon every year.

My personal best time was achieved during my fourth marathon, with a finish time of two hours and fifty-eight minutes. Come rain or shine, I remained committed to my running routine. I would brave all types of weather conditions, whether it was rainy, sunny, windy, or even snowy weather, enduring temperatures ranging from minus one degree Celsius to twenty. I had a few friends with whom I enjoyed running, playing golf, and tennis. Additionally, in the late evening hours, I would take my Jofa ice-skating shoes and indulge in some ice skating on the well-polished public ice-skating rink near my place. Ice skating was a skill I taught myself. Not wanting others to witness my falls, I would wait until it was dark and face my challenges alone, persisting until I became proficient at skating.

During Sana's travels or busy weekends, I took the opportunity to visit Are, a ski resort in the northern part of Sweden, on multiple occasions with my friends. Meanwhile, my cleaning company continued its operations, serving that specific client. However, around five years later, the company was sold to an American multinational corporation, which relocated the production to Mexico. Realizing that the cleaning services market had become saturated and prices were dropping, I made the decision not to seek another contract and subsequently deregistered the company. I chose to hold onto my regular warehouse job, which happened to be conveniently close to my home.

Being part of a large multinational corporation with thousands of employees and various departments, I recognized the potential for career growth and advancement within the organization. This became my workplace for the next seventeen years. Throughout my thirteen years of employment there, I never once arrived late or missed a day of work. I had established strong relationships with numerous people in my neighbourhood and surroundings, particularly with my closest neighbours. Everywhere I went, I endeavoured to display qualities of openness and humility. This approach translated well to my workplace, where I was equally well-known and respected by everyone, from the CEO to the cleaners. I approached my job with dedication, kindness, and a helpful demeanour, treating everyone equally.

Throughout my career, every manager I worked under consistently rated my performance highly. I have always been willing to go the extra mile not only to satisfy customers but also to ensure that teamwork thrives. I strive to be a creative worker, constantly generating ideas and strategies that benefit the company in both the short and long term, while also minimizing waste and ensuring proper management. It's worth noting that some colleagues have occasionally complained about my level of involvement, claiming that I take on too much. However, I believe it's crucial to fully embrace the terms and conditions of my work. After all, it is through my job that I earn a living and secure my survival, so I take it very seriously. Moreover, when the company succeeds, everyone benefits, starting with stable employment.

At a certain point in my life, I had what many would consider more than enough to feel content and joyful: a loving spouse, a car, a job I enjoyed, a spacious apartment, and engaging in meaningful voluntary work. However, that was not enough for me. I have always aimed higher and believed that the sky is the limit. I firmly believe that nothing is impossible until proven otherwise, and I never stop striving until I reach the top. As long as I maintain ambition, self-discipline, and unwavering determination, I know I can achieve my goals. I have made efforts to manage my time effectively, recognizing the importance of proper time management. In addition to my job, I diligently carried out voluntary work for my NGO, which involved tasks such as registering new members, collecting membership fees and donations, and handling correspondence. I am driven by the belief that there are no limits to what I can achieve, and I am committed to putting in the necessary effort to succeed.

I took great care in overseeing the various committees within the NGO, ensuring that they fulfilled their responsibilities. This included tasks such as distributing flyers, registering new members, and organizing sales events on Saturdays and sometimes Sundays at the local church, where we sold muffins and coffee. Another important fundraising activity was the sale of UNICEF Christmas cards, which took place every December in shopping malls and other public venues. The proceeds from these sales played a vital role in covering the monthly expenses of the orphanage. Although we received a portion of our annual budget from SIDA (Swedish International Development Cooperation Agency), it was never sufficient. SIDA tended to allocate more funding to projects in the southern part of Africa than other regions on the continent.

To ensure transparency and financial accountability, we developed a budget with the guidance of a certified accountant who was also a member of our organization. This budget was presented to the general body during the Annual General Meeting for confirmation before being submitted to SIDA along with a detailed report. There was always a continuous list of needs at the school, ranging from building repairs and furniture to rising food costs and clothing and shoes for the children. These additional expenses constantly required extra funds. However, we made it a priority to make the most of our limited resources, stretching every penny as far as possible. It was remarkable to see that almost seventy per cent of our NGO members were retirees who happily contributed their dues and made donations, understanding the significance of the work we were doing.

During our meetings, we created a warm and welcoming atmosphere where coffee and muffins were served, allowing everyone to socialize and get to know each other better. These gatherings fostered openness and liveliness among the group members. Additionally, we organized group visits to the orphanage in Ghana two to four times a year. These visits were not funded through the budget, but rather members gladly paid for their travel expenses. Many members would bring presents for the children, such as balls, candy, toys, and clothes. During these trips, two or three members were designated as auditors to ensure transparency and accountability.

After each visit, we held general discussions where members shared their observations, presented pictures and videos, and discussed the organization's current and future projects. We focused on making a positive impact on the children's lives, particularly in terms of their education. As there was always a high demand from other orphaned children seeking enrolment, we embarked on a modest expansion of the orphanage, taking into consideration our financial limitations. In collaboration with organizations like the Stockholm UN organization, SIDA, and the United Nations, we participated in meetings, conferences, and seminars on various UN issues. These included topics such as banning landmines, addressing refugee situations, eradicating extreme poverty, and promoting environmental sustainability. These issues were identified by the United Nations as crucial global agendas, and we were proud to contribute to these important discussions and initiatives.

This incident took place before the establishment of the Millennium Goals. There was a summer when I decided to spend my vacation in the United States, while Sana travelled to Moscow for a month. Sana had never shown any interest in exploring the USA; in fact, she had always avoided any involvement with the country. Upon my arrival at Baltimore Airport, I planned to drive to Washington, which was approximately a forty-minute car ride away. As I collected my luggage, a customs officer called me over for a random search. I placed my bags on the designated long table where searches typically took place and proceeded to open my large suitcase. The female officer inquired about the contents of my suitcase, to which I replied, "Nothing but my clothes, shoes, and a few Swedish candies for my friends."

She began to delve her hands into my suitcase, gradually removing each item and placing them on the table. Standing about a metre away from the table, I patiently waited as she continued the process of emptying my suitcase. Suddenly, she abruptly left and disappeared into a back room that was out of my sight. I remained there, waiting for her return to either finish emptying my suitcase or complete whatever task she had to attend to. As I stood waiting, ten minutes turned into twenty, and then thirty, with no sign of her or even a glimpse of her shadow. A colleague of hers approached me and inquired about the reason for my wait. I explained that his colleague, the lady officer, had been emptying my suitcase but had abruptly stopped and left. He furrowed his brow for a moment and responded, "She left a long time ago. You can go ahead and pack your things. You're free to leave now."

At that moment, I couldn't help but feel disappointed and at a loss for words to express my astonishment and frustration. However, I managed to stay calm. With a sense of bitterness, I packed my belongings and set off for Washington, DC. Despite the incident at the airport, the rest of my holiday turned out to be quite adventurous. I embarked on a road trip from Virginia to Florida, exploring various places along the way. I visited Shark Valley, Disney World, Miami Beach, the Everglades, and Kennedy Space Centre, and even made a stop in Charleston, South Carolina to see the plantations. Among the many interesting destinations, I also ventured up to Key West. Throughout my month-long journey, I thoroughly enjoyed immersing myself in the sights and experiences of the United States. However, indulgence in delicious food and exploration took its toll on my waistline, resulting in a weight gain of over six kilos.

Upon returning home around the same time as Sana, I saw she brought back a copy of the Pravda newspaper with a captivating front-page story. The story revolved around a man who had won a lottery ticket, which his wife discovered after his passing, but before the numbers were revealed. The lottery ticket had been in the pocket of her late husband's coat. Before his demise, the man had written the ticket number on a piece of paper and placed it on the kitchen fridge door using a magnet. When his wife saw the winning number, she concluded that the ticket must be in the coat pocket, as her husband was buried wearing that coat. She promptly reported the matter to the police, and the search for the lottery ticket began. To their surprise, upon exhuming the husband's grave, they discovered that the coffin was empty. The man's body was nowhere to be found. This unexpected turn of events added even more intrigue to the already fascinating story.

The widow provided detailed descriptions of the suit's colour and size, prompting the police to launch an investigation. Their first step was to visit second-hand clothing shops in search of the specific suit. After a couple of days, their efforts proved successful when they found the suit, with the winning ticket still inside the inner pocket, at a second-hand shop in central Moscow. The shop owner was subsequently arrested and interrogated. During their investigation, the police uncovered a mafia group operating in Moscow that engaged in disturbing practices. They would exhume fresh corpses, dismember them, sell the meat to restaurants, and sell the clothing to second-hand shops.

Curious about Sana's experiences during her trip, I asked if she had dined at any restaurants while in Moscow. Sana chuckled and reminded me of the restaurants we had visited together on our previous trip to the city. I decided not to dwell on the topic further. Apart from these unsettling incidents, we often spent time with our friend Karin, especially during the summer. It held great spiritual significance for Karin to visit Torsby every summer and lay flowers on her parents' graves. On occasion, we would accompany her, crossing the border to Norway to purchase items like goat cheese. Karin's youngest daughter, who was married to a policeman, also joined us frequently. We would go fishing together or simply enjoy each others' company, relishing the beauty of some of the world's most captivating natural sites.

During the early 1990s, a serial killer known as John Ausonius also referred to as "Lasermannen" or the laser man, terrorized Sweden by shooting and killing immigrants using a laser gun. The motivations behind his heinous acts remained known only to him. Subsequent investigations revealed that John Ausonius had a difficult upbringing. His family had relocated from Germany to Sweden, and he faced bullying and discrimination due to his dark hair and foreign background. This background of mistreatment contributed to his deep-seated self-hatred and animosity towards foreigners, as per psychological assessments. During that time, I received numerous sympathetic calls from concerned individuals, checking on my well-being. Karin, in particular, would cry every evening while watching the news reports as darkness fell and the laser man continued his rampage without being apprehended.

She would urge me to avoid going out, especially after dark. Being a black man, I would have been at great risk if I had encountered him. His attacks primarily targeted the Stockholm area, particularly around the University, where many international students resided. The city of Uppsala located an hour's drive from Stockholm, was also affected due to its large student population. Eventually, John Ausonius was arrested after injuring eleven people and causing the death of one individual. Racism and immigration have long been contentious topics in Swedish politics, often fuelled by right-wing media. Sweden did not have any organized body specifically dedicated to combating racism, apart from figures like Olof Palme, who openly spoke out against racism, oppression, and Western conflicts such as the Vietnam War and apartheid in South Africa.

Sweden, particularly through the Social Democratic Party, provided significant support to the African National Congress (ANC) in their fight against the South African regime. During Olof Palme's premiership, the Swedish government demonstrated generosity in aiding refugees and asylum seekers. However, in 1986, Palme was tragically assassinated in the heart of Stockholm while returning home from the movies. Speculation surrounding his murder has often suggested that his killer(s) held strong animosity towards his political views, leading to the assumption that the act was politically motivated, possibly originating from the right wing. Despite efforts involving cooperation from entities like the CIA and other intelligence agencies, the case remains unsolved.

While unions and left-leaning political parties in Sweden occasionally speak out against racism, discrimination, inequality, and integration issues, little progress has been made in terms of strengthening existing laws. These laws, in their current state, are deemed ineffective and lacking teeth. Many companies and employers in Sweden fail to promote or provide suitable job opportunities for minorities, resulting in reduced productivity, hindered growth, and limited diversity and creativity. Highly educated immigrants often face the discouraging response of being labelled "overqualified" during job selection processes. Consequently, individuals with backgrounds in fields such as medicine and engineering can be found working in low-skilled jobs like driving taxis or in factories, rather than being given opportunities for retraining within the job market. This wastage of human resources, talents, and productivity is primarily attributed to the lack of an effective integration policy by politicians, employers, and society as a whole.

The constant bashing and dehumanization of immigrants by right-wing media, as seen in Sweden and also in Denmark, is a dangerous recipe for future destabilization. Such rhetoric not only perpetuates discrimination and harm to individuals but also results in significant economic losses for society as a whole. Furthermore, the psychological and mental implications for the victims of racism are profound. Despite this, Sweden and even the European Union as a whole have yet to establish a political party or government with a comprehensive public policy that effectively combats racism and discrimination, treating all citizens equally. Europe's minorities continue to suffer in silence, as there is no European country that has successfully addressed the problem of racism.

Political representation for minorities remains extremely inadequate across all European countries. I know several individuals of African descent in Sweden who, even after graduating from university, have found themselves stuck in the lowest positions within companies for over fifteen years, despite their qualifications. They are often subjected to training others but are never given opportunities for promotion. In some instances, these individuals' faces are used for window-dressing diversity on the front office, brochures, and report covers, or for showcasing multiculturalism in advertisements. However, since racism is deeply ingrained in society, its eradication requires long-term and sustained efforts. A comprehensive and robust approach must be taken to address these issues, including systemic changes, educational programmes, and proactive measures to ensure equal opportunities for all citizens, regardless of their background. Only through such efforts can Europe truly strive towards a more inclusive and harmonious society.

Achieving a shift in attitudes within society is indeed crucial for fostering tolerance, acceptance, and respect for others. Some of my white friends would inquire about my experiences coping with racism and discrimination. While some felt ashamed and uncomfortable discussing the topic, they all shared the belief that racism and discrimination are unjustifiable and senseless. As I matured and gained a deeper understanding of Swedish society, I began setting boundaries by avoiding certain individuals, places, and conversations. This decision brought me a sense of peace. At my main job, where I had been working for several years, my colleagues knew me well. It was a significant milestone when my manager approached me and offered to lead the evening shift, which consisted of thirty people.

Having built a rapport with my colleagues over time, we frequently discussed work-related matters, including effective management strategies to enhance productivity and foster a more humane and harmonious work environment. I realized that my self-taught studies in management and leadership were paying off. With confidence in my abilities, I accepted the position and took charge of the team. Word quickly spread, and my promotion became a topic of discussion among many. My subordinates were competent and well-versed in their roles and responsibilities. Occasionally, I had to fill in for absent staff members by borrowing employees from other departments or establishing priorities to ensure smooth operations.

Ensuring the happiness, satisfaction, and motivation of the workforce was a top priority for me. I focused on creating a harmonious work environment by fostering cooperation, treating everyone equally, and actively listening to their input. Rather than giving strict commands and orders, I embraced a communication style that encouraged individual ownership of duties and responsibilities. It was crucial to respect each employee and value their skills and capabilities, as this contributed to the overall performance, smoothness, and effectiveness of our operations. We consistently completed assigned tasks and achieved our objectives during every shift.

However, my greatest challenge arose not within my department, but from managers in other departments who resisted the idea of me managing a department. The promotion of a foreigner, particularly a black man, to such a position had never happened before in the company's history. Other managers and division leaders would visit my department, engaging in conversations with my colleagues and seeking faults and errors that could be used against me. They would also inquire about the satisfaction of my colleagues with my leadership. Fortunately, my colleagues always exhibited high morale, energy, and willingness to work. They would come and share with me everything they heard or were asked. Despite the challenges posed by these external factors, the solidarity and support of my team remained unwavering. Their feedback and commitment to our shared goals played a vital role in overcoming the obstacles and maintaining a positive work environment.

Despite the challenges posed by the intrusive manager from another department, I stood my ground and asserted my autonomy. On two occasions, I firmly communicated to him that while I appreciated his willingness to help, I did not require lectures or instructions from him. Nevertheless, this manager persisted in engaging with my team members during breaks, seeking information and potential faults within my department. I was aware of these actions and became even more focused on avoiding errors. I chose to ignore him and remained dedicated to fulfilling my duties and responsibilities to the best of my abilities, prioritizing my relationships with my colleagues.

I took it upon myself to ensure that everything ran smoothly within the department. I arrived before anyone else, ensuring that everything was in order, and I was often the last to leave, ensuring that all necessary tasks were completed and the department was prepared for the next shift, ready to hit the ground running in the morning. I also dedicated significant effort to studying and understanding management and leadership, both in theory and practice. I recognized this opportunity as one that may not come my way again, so I seized it with determination, aiming to build a successful career in professional leadership. Other leaders who approached me with their problems and sought guidance often expressed surprise, wondering which prestigious school I had attended. I successfully led the evening shift for over two years, demonstrating my competence and effectiveness as a leader.

I maintained a positive working relationship with my manager, who was pleased with my performance. He valued my independence and freedom to lead the team, allowing me to make decisions and guide the staff effectively. Together, we displayed empathy and emotional intelligence skills by understanding and sympathizing with the situations our team members faced. The mentorship was an important aspect of our leadership approach, as we took a genuine interest in their development and provided counselling and support whenever needed (non-professional counselling). However, we also recognized the importance of assertiveness and made it clear when it was necessary to address issues or enforce expectations. Resolving complaints and grievances promptly and fairly was a priority for me, ensuring that issues were not allowed to linger and that judgments were made impartially, without favouritism or prejudice.

Similar to my childhood desire for order and cleanliness in my environment, I emphasized professionalism and organization in my responsibilities. I found that writing down reminders and creating a daily list of tasks helped me stay organized and focused. Treating everyone equally involved by asking questions, delegating tasks, providing opportunities for training and personal development, and fostering a sense of hope and motivation among the team members. I made sure that any available opportunities were communicated through notices on the information board, allowing everyone to express interest. Creating a harmonious work culture where different ideas were respected and encouraged was essential. However, it was important to avoid discussions about politics and religion in the workplace. Training and development programmes played a significant role in instilling hope and providing growth opportunities for the workers.

Maintaining open lines of communication within the department was a priority for me, as it encouraged engagement and the exchange of ideas among the team members. As a result, employees from other departments expressed their interest in joining my department. However, I discovered that there were specific criteria and genuine reasons for someone to be able to transfer from one department to another, which posed a challenge in accommodating these requests. Despite the challenges, I led the department with minimal friction and had a dedicated team that worked together to overcome obstacles and achieve the company's objectives. Sitting in my office with the team behind me, I sometimes felt a sense of disbelief at how my life had changed. It was a reminder that life can change rapidly and in unexpected ways.

Contributing to the well-being of children in the orphanage filled me with pride and gave me hope for their future. The extreme poverty, misery, and suffering that I witnessed both personally and through the news were disheartening. At times, I felt overwhelmed by the enormity of Africa's problems and doubted if they could be solved within my lifetime. However, my perspective shifted when I had the opportunity to attend a conference in Stockholm where I met a social scientist named Hans Rosling. He presented evidence that the developing world, including Africa, has been progressing at a faster rate than the Western world did during its development. His insights provided hope and suggested that Africa has the potential to experience unimaginable development within a few decades.

Hans Rosling's programme model and his lectures provided valuable insights into the development trajectory of high-income countries and how similar progress could be achieved in Africa. As a genius professor of global health at Sweden's Karolinska Teaching Institute, his expertise and global reach, including speaking at the United Nations, made a significant impact. He demonstrated how poverty eradication, education, a reduction in child mortality, and family planning were rapidly progressing in Africa. Listening to Hans Rosling speak at the conference filled me with hope and reaffirmed my commitment to making a difference in the lives of the children in the orphanage. His message inspired me to continue my efforts, believing that a brighter future was possible for them.

Throughout a couple of decades, I have witnessed positive changes in Africa's development. The middle class is growing, more Africans are pursuing higher education, and infrastructure development is taking place at a rapid pace across the continent. Democratic processes are becoming more prevalent, with an increase in free and fair elections. However, it is important to note that despite these improvements, the lingering perception in the West of war, starvation, and disease in Africa from the past persists in the subconscious of many. Humanitarian organizations from the West used to provide significant aid to Africa, but the need for such assistance has significantly reduced over time, indicating progress and self-sustainability.

Africans must select leaders who demonstrate unwavering commitment and implement effective public policies. It is crucial to establish robust and transparent institutions that are free from corruption and inefficiency. Africa had the potential to surpass its current state if it had approached the post-independence era in the 1960s with the right perspective. Despite having well-educated individuals capable of leading Africa effectively, the continent's progress is impeded by weak institutions, widespread corruption, and a lack of transparency. Even though I maintain optimism for the children in the orphanage, it cannot be denied that they will face significant challenges in securing decent employment and building families.

Unemployment and social unrest pose the greatest challenges for African governments unless substantial investments are made in youth training, development, and employment in the short, medium, and long terms. It is crucial to establish skill centres, training institutions, and programmes that overhaul the education system and equip children with skills, entrepreneurship, innovation, self-sufficiency, as well as moral and ethical values. The current education system in African schools primarily focuses on producing employees who earn meagre wages, which do not contribute to their overall development, especially in the context of limited job opportunities. Africa possesses a young and dynamic, yet impoverished population, which poses a potential time bomb of social unrest for any government.

In the coming decades, Africa's trajectory will be a refreshing sight to behold, as the continent steers towards democracy, development, good governance, and the rule of law. This transformation will occur alongside a better-educated and youthful population equipped with powerful tools like the internet and social media, residing in a global village. The world we live in today is vastly different from what it was merely two decades ago. African politicians must recognize that traditional methods of conducting politics and engaging in leadership contests have evolved. Many young Africans are actively engaged in shaping government policies, demanding greater transparency and accountability from their leaders, more so than ever before.

While Sweden may be perceived by some as a predominantly homogeneous society, it is a multicultural nation, albeit with minority populations often concentrated in urban suburbs. The country boasts a well-organized, cultivated, and modern environment, supported by strong institutions. The Swedish system offers numerous opportunities and avenues for individuals to strive and succeed, encapsulating what is often referred to as the "Swedish Dream". Various job options, educational pathways, and other prospects are accessible to anyone who desires them. Every aspect of Swedish society is structured to incorporate bureaucratic elements that serve as checks and balances, enhancing efficiency, preventing corruption, and minimizing mistakes, faults, oversights, and wastage.

Many individuals express concerns about excessive bureaucracy and the presence of checks and balances. However, I do not worry about these aspects. I strongly believe in routines and structures that uphold order, good governance, and efficiency. Such a system also fosters a commitment to transparency and accountability, which I greatly value. Swedish society and its way of life differ from any other place I have known or experienced. Nonetheless, it is a system that I admire as it aligns well with my natural inclinations and lifestyle. I have encountered situations where my Swedish friends and colleagues, whether at school or work, have remarked that I embody a more Swedish mindset than the native Swedes themselves. While I found this comment somewhat insulting, I have always stayed true to myself and never attempted to copy or imitate anyone. This is simply who I am by nature, and I feel safe within my comfort zone. I find contentment in my culture and traditions, just as I do with other cultures. I am always eager to learn about and understand the norms and characteristics of different cultures. While there may be certain aspects of my own culture that I dislike, I refrain from complaining. The same goes for any other culture, as there may be elements that some find undesirable, but I never criticize or admonish them. Karin used to tell me that I was born with a Swedish attitude, and my response has always been that it's all a result of my nature and how my Mum raised me.

Nevertheless, it was important for me to learn about and familiarize myself with Swedish culture and traditions to integrate successfully. There are certain Swedish dishes that I genuinely enjoy, such as meatballs, lingonberry sauce, kalops (a meat stew with spices and potatoes), pea soup with pancakes, and herring, which is a widely popular fish. Swedes generally prefer a balanced approach and are averse to anything extreme. As the saying goes, "moderation is best!" The majority of people are well-mannered, down-to-earth, and kind-hearted. However, it is essential to acknowledge that no society is perfect, including Sweden.

There are certain aspects of Swedish society that I disapprove of. For instance, Swedish snus, which involves placing moist tobacco under the lower or upper lip, is something I find unfavourable. While alcohol is readily available in Swedish society, its sale and exposure are still regulated. Smoking was widespread in the 1980s but has rapidly fallen out of fashion since the 1990s. These are just a few examples of things I don't particularly like. Additionally, I have observed a sense of self-centeredness, discourtesy, and a lack of respect for others among some individuals, especially among the younger generation, which can be detrimental to any society. The importance of upholding good moral values for the betterment of society seems to have diminished among Swedish youths.

There have been ongoing debates among social scientists in Sweden regarding whether figures like Pippi Longstocking should be banned due to their perceived influence on society. Pippi Longstocking is a strong, powerful girl character who defies conventions and pushes boundaries and is widely popular among children through TV shows and books. Some argue that her presence challenges social cohesion and hampers the ability to maintain relationships, particularly marriages, as well as society's overall capacity to care for and support one another. It is believed that a lack of human emotion is prevalent in the younger generation. Sweden is a highly capitalistic modern society where self-centredness, ego, wealth, and success often take centre stage for individuals. This emphasis on personal gain has led to the freedom to treat others disrespectfully and a lack of consideration for others. Consequently, this has resulted in a sense of coldness and deeply ingrained selfish behaviour that can be challenging for outsiders to comprehend and adapt to.

While these characteristics and attitudes are not ones that immigrants necessarily need to embrace or assimilate, some Swedes and political parties argue that immigrants should adopt these behaviours called Swedish values to be seen as integrated and assimilated. However, I disagree with this notion. Despite the aforementioned traits, Sweden is a vast and stable country with less-than-ideal weather conditions. Swedes, for the most part, are shy and reserved individuals. Despite their self-centredness, there are still many Swedes especially the old ones who demonstrate sympathy, empathy, and solidarity towards the weak, poor, and vulnerable. As you move further north in the country, people tend to be even quieter. I was able to smoothly assimilate and integrate into Swedish society without encountering significant difficulties, aside from occasional instances of racism.

Living in a structured and organized society like Sweden has always suited me well, and I am grateful for the choice I made to live there. Since childhood, I have always strived to abide by the laws and uphold order, regardless of the circumstances. This commitment has helped me maintain a clean record and never break the law, no matter where I have lived. My attitude towards money and finance has always been to only make purchases that I can afford. I have never been swayed or tempted to take out loans, even when friends around me were flaunting their latest cars and luxurious homes. Despite my team and I performing well, achieving good productivity figures through hard work and dedication, news reached me that a US multinational Food corporation had acquired our company and another Norwegian partner company. Soon after the merger, changes began to take place within the company.

The corporate language shifted from Swedish to English, a new CEO was appointed, and significant changes in the workplace were on the horizon. This created a sense of nervousness among employees, leading to daily rumours and gossip. Unfortunately, I had no information regarding what would happen within my department. Colleagues approached me with questions that I was unable to answer. But, despite the uncertainty, we continued to excel in our work, maintaining high morale and meeting our daily targets. However, it was later revealed that my section would be shut down and relocated to Oslo, Norway within a couple of months. We were to be assigned to different departments, and I would lose my leadership position in the process.

Receiving such news was undoubtedly difficult to digest. However, as a leader, it was essential for me to maintain composure, remain calm, and move forward. I called for a meeting to address the situation, which was a sombre but brief gathering. The team had questions about our future, such as where we would be placed and whether our wages would remain the same. I answered their queries to the best of my ability, explaining that the department's relocation to Norway was not a result of poor performance but rather a cost-cutting measure introduced by the new owner. Unfortunately, the most unfortunate consequence was that our team would disperse, with close friends being assigned to different departments.

The dissolution of the camaraderie we had developed over time was a sorrowful occurrence. In my final speech, I encouraged everyone to be grateful for the opportunity to continue serving the company. I expressed my belief that things would work out for each individual, even though we would only occasionally see each other at work. I reminded them that everyone faces difficulties in life and finds ways to overcome them. Transitioning to a new department was not the end of the world; we would have the chance to meet and work with new colleagues, and life would go on. However, a couple of weeks later, we discovered that more than a third of the entire workforce had either been laid off with compensation or offered early retirement. There was a sentiment circulating among employees that "things will never be the same again in this company" with the arrival of the Americans!

Following the closure of my department and its relocation to Norway, there were extensive discussions and negotiations between the company and the strong workers' union. Eventually, the situation began to stabilize. However, the remaining employees faced an increased workload, leading to distress and unhappiness among everyone. In my case, I was transferred to another department, specifically the central warehouse, as a regular worker, a small department but called the heart of the company. This department is in charge of storage, sales and distribution. It was a significant change from my previous leadership position. I remember two managers approaching me and asking how it felt to no longer be leading a department. Although it felt like a mockery comment, I tried to maintain a positive outlook and expressed gratitude for still having a job rather than being laid off.

Karin, my Swedish guardian, was unhappy about my loss of a prestigious position and urged me to leave the company and find a better job elsewhere. However, I hesitated due to the potential challenges I might face as a black man in the job market. It's always more difficult to secure a job. I didn't want to become another statistic of unemployment. However, I believed that remaining in the company provided opportunities for advancement, considering its size and potential. Unfortunately, my first few weeks in the new department were deeply upsetting. I encountered racism from day one. Two co-workers objected to my transfer to the department. The department with significant importance, which has a history of staff members who had been there for twenty to thirty years could welcome me rather than these individuals making my transition difficult.

I expressed my shock and disappointment when the two colleagues openly expressed their racist views and objected to my presence there. I remained calm and composed in the face of their offensive remarks. Recognizing the seriousness of the situation, I decided to contact my first-line manager and inform him about the matter. To my surprise, he acknowledged that he was aware of these individuals' racist views and tendencies, especially one of them. He admitted that they had caused trouble for every immigrant, foreigner or anyone with a different skin colour in the department.

I emphasized to my manager that it was his responsibility as the leader of the department to ensure a stable and inclusive working environment, free from harassment, discrimination, and racism. He needed to prioritize the security and safety of all employees and promote a workplace with harmony, high standards, and opportunities for everyone to thrive.

I suggested that a letter of warning should be issued to the two colleagues to address their behaviour. Before I left the manager's office, two other colleagues noticed the conversation and approached me, inquiring about the matter at hand.

I shared with them the details of the racist remarks I encountered from the two individuals I came across. These two individuals, who identified themselves as representatives of the Union, assured me that they would support and protect me from any racism within the department. I mentioned that I had been a member of the Union for several years and intended to remain one, as it was a common practice among most people. They decided to escalate the issue by filing a grievance case and arranging a meeting with my manager to address the situation. The following day, an investigation was initiated, during which I provided a detailed account of what transpired, including the time, location, and events involved.

After a week, I received the news that the two individuals had only received a verbal warning. There were speculations that our manager, who happened to be German, would always take their side, which seemed to divide the department into two factions: the supportive and the unsupportive. However, our manager didn't take the matter seriously and let it slip by quietly. Despite the negative attitude of those two colleagues towards me from the beginning, I managed to build a positive rapport within the department. I was dedicated, friendly, and always willing to assist others, diligently fulfilling my responsibilities while avoiding any conflicts, especially with my adversaries.

Our department was highly coveted by many people due to its unique attributes. It boasted a small workforce, granting individuals a sense of autonomy in their roles, and offered higher wages compared to other departments. Outsiders often inquired about how I managed to secure a position there and who facilitated the negotiation process on my behalf. Our department held control over the entire storage, sales, distribution and supply chain, making it a highly influential entity. Despite transitioning from a managerial role in another department to a regular worker, I was grateful to have been considered for this esteemed department, especially considering the higher level of wages there. I embraced the opportunity and quickly familiarized myself with the new advanced warehouse software system SAP.

During the early 1990s, our warehouse department ranked as the fifth largest in Europe and most technologically advanced. It showcased cutting-edge technology, providing a clean and bright environment where robots and electronic tools efficiently carried out tasks, ensuring a seamless supply chain operation. Thanks to our state-of-the-art technology, we welcomed a significant number of visitors from around the world every week, particularly from Japan, Germany, and the USA, who sought to observe our amazing system in action. Working in such a prestigious department filled us all with a sense of pride. I continued to handle my job comfortably while effectively managing my involvement in an NGO and pursuing various other activities on the side. However, as time passed, the cost-cutting measures implemented after the company takeover began to take their toll.

The decline in productivity became apparent as fewer employees were willing to work overtime. Motivation and morale among workers plummeted, leading to the development of tensions, resentment, and chaos throughout the workplace. Customer complaints regarding delayed product deliveries began to escalate. Productivity took a significant hit, resulting in declining profits for the quarter. The work environment suddenly became toxic, marked by heightened tensions and increased absenteeism, leading to a drastic drop in production figures company-wide. The strained relationship between management and workers, influenced by the clash between an American management style that focuses on profit maximization and Sweden's heavily unionized environment, exacerbated stress and anxiety.

In Sweden, a country where employees are well aware of their rights, the balance between employer and employee is sought, ensuring equality and the importance of every single worker. When conflicts arise in the workplace, it is ultimately the customers who suffer the consequences, and they may choose to take their business elsewhere or to the competitor if dissatisfied. Losing long-term customers has detrimental effects on the business, highlighting the importance of retaining existing customers rather than constantly seeking new ones. Consequently, top management found themselves dedicating more time to conflict resolution than focusing on work-related matters.

Escalating tensions, conflicts, and a general reluctance to collaborate among production unit personnel became increasingly infectious and widespread. As a result, the company decided to bring in a management consultant to investigate the issues and provide recommendations for resolution. At this point, I realized that I needed to voice my thoughts on the matter and propose potential solutions. In my assessment, the primary problem seemed to stem from a deficiency in management and leadership. Consequently, conducting a comprehensive overhaul of the company's middle management division appeared to be the only viable solution. Without addressing this issue, chaos would persist, employee satisfaction would remain low, and productivity would continue to suffer.

Within our IT system, there existed an intranet platform that facilitated the sharing of ideas, discussion of work-related matters, and brainstorming for the betterment of the company. I thought that this platform presented an ideal opportunity for me to articulate substantive ideas and gauge the opinions of others. Every Friday, I decided to resolve to compose well-structured and concise articles, written in both English and Swedish, outlining potential solutions to the existing problems. I chose not to inform anyone in advance about my intention to start contributing articles to this idea platform. The first article was published on a Friday afternoon, employing simplified language and presenting ideas in a clear and well-formulated manner in concise and short paragraphs.

I diligently ensured that the articles published every Friday revolved around the theme of effective leadership. I discussed topics such as establishing a credible and authoritative relationship between leaders and employees, strategies for motivating employees to achieve set goals, and the characteristics of the modern workforce compared to the past. Additionally, I delved into leadership qualities and functions, organizational behaviour, the Japanese management approach, and the benefits of a flat organizational structure. In these articles, I provided reasonable recommendations and proposals, outlining the actions that the company should take to regain its footing, increase productivity, and foster a harmonious working environment, ultimately creating a win-win situation for all.

Unbeknownst to me, top officials within the company were reading my articles. It was a pleasant surprise when I first encountered a group of top bosses outside our department one day who expressed their appreciation for my writing, describing it as outstanding. As we stood there, some were curious to know which school I had attended.

On the other hand, my adversaries, the two individuals who had made racist remarks, started making statements suggesting that my writing would never lead to a top position within the company. Colleagues approached me and informed me about these comments. I made it clear to them that my intention was never to pursue a top job within the company or anywhere else. I emphasized that I was simply sharing my ideas on how to reform the company for the benefit of everyone, which aligned with the main purpose of the intranet forum — to encourage contributions and ideas from all employees.

As I continued to write, my ideas gained more attention and sparked discussions among colleagues. However, this increased visibility also intensified hostility coming from the two adversaries. After so many months working there, they expressed a desire to investigate the circumstances surrounding my transfer to the department, questioning whether it was done correctly. In response, the Union firmly stood by my side, making it clear to them that such matters were none of their concern. I took pride in writing in English, knowing that it was a language well-understood by the top officials. There were International officials from Switzerland and the USA who were fluent and proficient in English.

As the corporate language shifted to English, more English speakers joined the office. Recognizing this, I realized that my English language skills could serve as a valuable asset to further my career within the company. It became apparent that neither my line manager nor most of my colleagues were able to express themselves in English beyond a few basic words or phrases. Interestingly, my writings gained popularity among the higher echelons of the company. The CEO, whom I prefer not to mention by name in this account, started visiting our department on Friday evenings. During these visits, he was guided around by our line manager, and he expressed appreciation to everyone in the department.

The following Friday, the CEO once again visited our department and made his way to my workstation. I introduced myself, and he immediately asked if I was the one writing the articles on the intranet. I confirmed that I was, and he expressed his appreciation, stating that he found them interesting and valuable in offering useful and constructive ideas. This interaction left me delighted and confident, knowing that he was indeed reading my postings. Two Fridays later, the CEO made another visit to our section and inquired about the progress of our work. We engaged in a conversation for approximately fifteen minutes before he departed. Shortly after he left, my line manager approached me and asked what the CEO had said. I informed him that our conversation was nothing out of the ordinary, mostly discussing the company in general rather than anything concerning our department.

In response, my line manager cautioned me to be careful about what I shared with the CEO. I reassured him, stating that if the CEO ever asked about our department, I would direct him to speak with him as the manager and my immediate boss. I emphasized that if I had nothing positive to say about the department, I would prefer to remain silent. However, my manager was displeased that the CEO had visited our department and only engaged in conversation with me and left. This made me contemplate the potential repercussions of the situation. The same experience from my former job started to kick into my brain. Once my manager left looking serious, my colleagues began approaching me, inquiring about the conversation with the CEO. I explained the nature of our discussion, and one colleague jokingly asked if I was becoming friends with the top boss. I clarified that I had never invited him to visit me or initiated any personal relationship.

During another CEO's visit, we engaged in a short conversation about the company. I then took the opportunity to ask him some personal questions about family, work experience, education etc. However, it was nothing more than a casual exchange. On that particular Friday, I decided to write an article addressing the relationship between leaders and employees, focusing on the importance of avoiding tension and the role of motivation in boosting productivity. Although no specific names or departments were mentioned, the article described common problems within the company and how to overcome them. The hierarchical structure of the organization, resembling a pyramid model, often resulted in friction, resentment and conflicts.

I expressed my belief that section managers held excessive unchecked powers, which were frequently misused. Unfortunately, this article proved to be unpopular among line managers. Complaints were lodged to my line manager later that day. I discussed the situation with him, reminding him of the ongoing issues that the CEO addresses in various departments. I highlighted the fact that a management consultant had been hired to investigate and provide recommendations for resolving these problems. Failing to address these issues could potentially jeopardize all of our jobs. Therefore, I stressed that my intention was simply to offer advice and suggestions on how to improve the situation for the benefit of everyone.

During another visit, I had a conversation with the CEO, I inquired about his thoughts on an article I had written regarding corporate organizational structure. In the article, I proposed recommendations to transition from a pyramid to a flat organizational structure. This new structure aimed to eliminate middle management, streamline decision-making processes, and empower workers to take ownership and feel motivated which will increase productivity. To my delight, the CEO responded positively, stating that a special committee was actively considering such an option. He further expressed appreciation for my articles, assuring me that they were indeed being followed. At that moment, I couldn't help but feel a surge of excitement and validation. It seemed like I had been encouraged to continue writing about corporate leadership and management, knowing that the top echelon of the company was paying attention. This recognition elevated my profile within the company.

Despite the newfound attention, I remained composed and avoided any conflicts or troubles with others, regardless of any provocation. I continued to carry out my duties diligently, with unwavering dedication and passion. A couple of months later, during a general meeting, it was announced that significant changes were imminent, potentially resulting in the elimination of numerous positions and personnel. Unfortunately, even those who had been with the company for decades might be affected. The changes had reached a stage where there was no turning back. Negotiations with the Union and other stakeholders had already been finalized, and the process was set in motion.

After the meeting where the impending changes were announced, I had a sense of what might transpire, particularly that certain line managers and other leadership positions could be eliminated. The following Friday, I wrote a concise article consisting of three paragraphs, focusing on how to effectively manage organizational changes. Some line managers started pointing fingers at me for being responsible for their potential job losses. I was taken aback by their claims and questioned where such ideas originated. I firmly believed that I hadn't done anything that caused any job loss for anyone, but shared ideas I knew would bring sanity to the company. The purpose of the intranet platform was to encourage idea-sharing and learning from one another. I maintained a clear conscience, as I refrained from targeting specific individuals or naming any department.

Despite my line manager not being fond of my writing endeavours, we maintained a respectful relationship. I understood that he would occasionally make comments whenever I wrote in Swedish, but I also knew that someone was translating the articles for him. Meanwhile, my two adversaries grew increasingly frustrated with my actions and stance. They launched personal attacks against our line manager, asserting that I would bring about the downfall of the company, and we would all suffer the consequences. They claimed that he had made a grave mistake by accepting me into the department. I became aware of an argument they had with him, during which they even suggested that I should be transferred elsewhere to another department.

I would not have agreed to transfer to another department unless I had either made a mistake or felt dissatisfied with my work. Except for those two colleagues, I had a positive rapport with everyone. However, my relationship with my line manager was not simply bad but rather complicated. I firmly believe in avoiding discussions about politics or religion in the workplace. There are individuals whose beliefs may clash with corporate policies, culture, regulations, and values. It is wiser to remain silent than to express opinions that may offend others. One afternoon, my manager approached me discreetly and made a shocking statement, proclaiming, "You know, I think Hitler was a good man; people just misunderstood him!" He swiftly departed, leaving me stunned.

Rather than responding, I watched him depart, clutching a stack of papers, in utter disbelief. I chose not to share this incident with anyone and did not take offence, assuming it was simply his personal belief. Since he had not discriminated against me or treated me unfairly, I decided to dismiss that outrageous remark. Exercising patience and tolerance is crucial. Reacting impulsively can often be counterproductive or even detrimental if one is not careful. If one were to confront such racist remarks, it is better to take time and respond thoughtfully and appropriately. Some situations can provoke and potentially damage one's career. It is essential to maintain relationships and foster understanding with others. Despite this incident, I continued to support the department by working overtime whenever necessary to ensure timely order fulfilment for our customers.

Anticipation grew among both managers and employees as speculation about potential changes continued to circulate in the company. The management consultant concluded their investigation and released a final report, which was summarized and posted on the information board. The complete report could be obtained from the main office. During the consultation process, staff from all departments were interviewed anonymously to gauge their level of satisfaction with management/leadership and their work environment. Unfortunately, the results were predominantly negative across all departments. The managers, particularly, began to feel vulnerable, concerned that the report might recommend reforms that could jeopardize their positions, especially for those who had been abusing their authority.

This apprehension led to a sudden shift in many managers' behaviour, displaying a surprising change in attitude that caught everyone off guard. Subsequently, a list was published outlining which managers would be leaving or transferring to other roles, along with details of the new structural changes being implemented. Fortunately, the changes aligned with my expectations. All managerial positions were eliminated, resulting in some managers being made redundant while others opted for early retirement. Team leadership roles were also abolished and replaced with new supervisor positions, which were made available for anyone to apply. I came to understand that some former team leaders successfully transitioned into supervisory positions within their respective departments after undergoing the application process.

However, some former managers perceived the newly introduced supervisor positions as lower in rank compared to their previous roles, and as a result, they showed no interest in pursuing them. This sentiment fuelled various rumours, speculations, and conspiracy theories that circulated throughout the organization. Some managers believed it was more dignified to leave the company on their terms rather than accept a lower position, reminiscent of my own experience when my department was closed. Coincidentally, our department manager opted for early retirement, thereby creating an opening for a supervisor to lead the department. Everything unfolded rapidly, with all those who were leaving the company departing within a couple of weeks.

Our manager, who had dedicated 25 years to the organization, expressed exhaustion and eagerness to embark on a new chapter in life. This sparked widespread speculation about who would succeed him in the role. There was thorough scrutiny and attention directed towards prominent individuals, particularly those positioned higher up in the hierarchy, who were considered potential contenders for top positions. Other leaders from different departments, who had worked closely with our manager and department, expressed interest in assuming the role to replace him.

A few days later, a union colleague approached me and asked if I was interested in the supervisor position, noting that I had previously successfully led a department. We shared a laugh about it, and I responded, "Never. Even if I were to apply, I doubt I would be considered for a position of this calibre. It's beyond my reach." We brushed it off as a lighthearted conversation. However, a week later, on a Friday evening before closing time, our CEO unexpectedly visited the workplace. He made his way around the office and eventually reached my desk. I took the opportunity to congratulate him on the commendable job he had done with the reform project and the impressive report. I mentioned that the implementation phase, including the appointment of new supervisors, was the next crucial step. Just as he was about to leave, he remarked, "But I haven't seen your application for your department yet. Have a great weekend," and departed. I was left perplexed, wondering about his comment.

Shortly after the CEO's departure, as per usual, my manager approached me and inquired about the conversation. I responded, "Nothing much, just me congratulating him on the challenging work they have undertaken in the report and reform programme." My manager nodded and remarked, "Alright, so it means you support the ongoing changes, even when many people are losing their jobs— some of whom have dedicated almost two to three decades to this company." I clarified that I wasn't the one initiating the changes that led to job losses and added that we were all aware of the chaos within departments that necessitated the intervention of a consultant. The prevailing resentment, tension, and grievances across almost every department were unhealthy and unacceptable.

My thoughts about the reform process became irrelevant. Over the weekend, I dedicated my time to rewriting my CV for the position of supervisor of our department. I kept my application a secret from Sana, Karin, and everyone else at work. Sometimes, my thoughts about the position conflicted with each other on whether or not to go ahead and apply. It was a high-level role with extensive responsibilities encompassing the entire sales, distribution and supply chain, overseeing employees, coordinating logistics, managing quality, handling customers, and overseeing documentation in Europe's fifth-largest warehouse. Despite my conflicting thoughts, I decided to go for it. On Monday, while heading to the restaurant, I dropped off my CV at the reception desk. I addressed the envelope to the CEO's Assistant and included a small note inside for the CEO himself. And he received it.

A couple of hours later, my phone rang while my manager stood next to my desk. It was the CEO on the line. He informed me that he had received my CV and would review it and pass it over to HR. Unfortunately, my manager overheard the conversation and inquired about the caller. I casually replied, "The big boss," and chuckled. Curious, he asked, "Which big boss?" to which I disclosed the CEO's name. This sparked assumptions among everyone that I had a good relationship with the CEO. My manager expressed surprise, saying, "Look, I've been working here for over 25 years, and no CEO has ever called me."

As a result of the phone call from the CEO, my enemies grew angrier with me but also became more cautious in their interactions. The call became the talk of the department that week, with some colleagues curious about the reason behind it. However, I couldn't disclose that it was related to my CV and application for a supervisory position. I feared that sharing this information would only invite hostility and potential attempts to sabotage my application. To navigate this situation, I chose to keep silent about the CEO's call. I focused on performing my work to the best of my ability, neither revealing nor concealing anything related to the conversation.

Later, I learned from the CEO's Assistant that the HR department was processing my CV. Around the middle of the following week, our CEO unexpectedly visited our department and encountered me outside the office. We exchanged kind words and shared a jovial moment. Amid our conversation, he posed a direct question, asking if I believed I could effectively manage the department. Without hesitation, I replied spontaneously, "Oh yes, without a doubt. I can do it even better than you think." With that, he departed without saying another word. Two of my colleagues approached me, perplexed by the brief encounter, and asked if he had simply stopped by to say hello. I casually responded, "Oh no, he was just passing through," downplaying the significance of the interaction.

One observation I've made about many Swedes, although not applicable to everyone, is that despite their strong values of peace, liberalism, and democracy, along with their possession of various rights, they tend to display a respectful demeanour and often avoid direct interactions with their top bosses. In my case, however, it's quite the opposite. I believe that top bosses can always offer valuable lessons. They are human beings like anyone else, but with their high positions, and extensive experience, they can serve as mentors, coaches, and sources of wisdom and support.

There is much to be gained from others. Moreover, what often brings people together and fosters genuine interest is the discovery of shared values, ideas and commonalities. Fortunately, I find that I have many things in common with my people wherever I go. I always try to facilitate meaningful relationships with people and try to build bridges. Perhaps this inclination has been with me since childhood, as most of my friends used to be older than me and I felt secure around them. Additionally, I give credit to my beloved Mum for instilling in me essential human qualities that have shaped my perspective.

The body language I received from our CEO during his last visits instilled a strong belief within me that I had a high likelihood of securing the desired position. Consequently, my mind became filled with thoughts of the actions I would take, the potential impact on my future career, my communication skills, my relationships with the workers and the Union, and how I could establish myself as the department's best leader. Drawing upon my knowledge and understanding of management and leadership, I realized that the time had come to put my expertise into practice.

I recognized that it was the perfect opportunity to demonstrate my professionalism and implement the articles and recommendations I had previously shared on the Intranet platform. I understood that some leaders might have felt challenged in their positions due to my writings, so it was important for me to perform at an even higher level to prove myself if I should secure the position. However, deep within my subconscious, there had always been a subtle persuasion that one day I might find myself in a leadership position, and now I felt that the time had finally arrived. I held trust and confidence in myself, possessing the necessary knowledge and capabilities to succeed in any leadership role. Two weeks later, on a Friday, I received an invitation from the HR office to attend a meeting in the main meeting room. I learned that I was the only one from our department who was invited, heightening my anticipation of what lay ahead.

As I made my way to the meeting, I mentally prepared myself for what I believed would be an interview, contemplating the appropriate questions and answers for the position. Upon arrival, I encountered a few familiar faces, causing me to wonder how we would all undergo interviews within the allotted time. Someone in the group mentioned that they had already gone through our interviews the previous week. Curiosity piqued, I decided to wait and see what would unfold. Soon, our CEO and the Director of HR entered the room, marking the beginning of the meeting. As the presentation lit up on the screen, I noticed my name and department followed by the statement, "You are the new departmental leaders called Supervisors." It was at that moment I realized that I am indeed the new leader of our department.

The CEO further elucidated the new organizational structure, emphasizing a flat hierarchy. We were entrusted with the duties, responsibilities, and obligations of being dedicated, fair, and hardworking leaders for the benefit of the company and the people we would be guiding. After the one-hour meeting, the HR Director would conduct quick introductory sessions with the new supervisors in their respective departments. However, my session was scheduled for Monday. Filled with a sense of pride and confidence, I completed my work for the evening and left, eager to share the news with Sana during dinner. The revelation turned our dinner into a joyous celebration. We spent the rest of the evening immersed in happiness. The following day, when Karin and I met for coffee, she also learned about my new position and joined in the excitement.

I the news of my promotion with my family, they congratulated me and offered their good wishes, but also cautioned me to be vigilant as there may be those who would try to undermine my success. Arriving at work on Monday, I anticipated witnessing our manager's farewell, only to realize that I had missed his departure remarks on Friday. Soon after, the HR director arrived and swiftly called for a brief meeting in the early morning. All the employees gathered, and without hesitation, he announced, "Now you have a new leader," as he called out my name. The room fell into complete silence, taken aback by the unexpected revelation. The HR director continued, stating that there was no need for him to introduce me as I was already well-known among the team.

Suddenly, one of my adversaries, the individual with racist views, erupted in a loud voice, vehemently objecting, "Not in my name! How could you all do this? This guy has only been here for less than a year, and now he will be our leader. We have dedicated two or three decades to this company! What is the company thinking?" It was evident from the body language of others that some were inclined to agree with his remarks. In response, the HR director firmly requested that he refrain from using such a tone, advising him to channel any complaints or grievances through the appropriate channels, either through the company or the Union. As he left the room, he extended his congratulations and wished me good luck. The women in the office approached me, one by one, offering their congratulations. In an attempt to ease the tension, I suggested we continue with our breakfast break and take an additional fifteen minutes.

I decided to brew another pot of coffee while the secretary pondered over the bewildering situation. "Well," I spoke up. "It has happened, so let's adapt and work diligently. We all share the common goal of performing well and benefitting the company." The two colleagues with racist tendencies continued to grumble and vent as they stormed out of the office, threatening to take the matter to the Union. Others remained silent but were surprised that I had taken charge. The entire incident caught everyone off guard. However, someone mentioned, "If your case goes to the Union, they will scrutinize whether you obtained the job rightfully or not."

I replied, "Listen, the job vacancy was advertised for over a week, and I was the only one who applied." Another person interjected, "Oh, you applied for the position? I don't think so. We noticed that the CEO frequently visited you and had discussions. Something was going on." I emphasized that if they believed there was an issue with my appointment, they were welcome to complain to the Union. Soon after, we all dispersed. The secretary reassured me, saying, "Don't mind them. They're just jealous, and those two never liked you anyway." My intention wasn't to be liked, but rather to be respected, fostering teamwork to achieve the company's goals and objectives. The two individuals with racist attitudes left the department without my authorization.

After going to the Union's office to discuss my appointment, the two colleagues returned nearly half an hour later. Since it was my first day as a department leader, I chose to ignore their presence and focused on avoiding any conflicts. However, it was apparent that they had no intention of working that day. Instead, they spent their time in the cafeteria, engaging in conversations with everyone around them. Consequently, very little progress was made in the morning, as I was occupied with setting up my new office space. I noticed that the employees were segregating themselves into discussion groups rather than dedicating themselves to their tasks. Around two in the afternoon, the secretary approached me and delivered disheartening news: everyone was refusing to work and staging a protest against my leadership. My heart sank, my blood rushed faster through my veins, and I started perspiring, all while trying to maintain a composed smile.

Initially, I believed it was some sort of prank, but upon observing the lack of productivity throughout the morning and witnessing ongoing group discussions, I realized the seriousness of the situation. I decided to approach them in the cafeteria or breakroom and calmly inquired, "May I know what's going on, please?" An infuriated individual, who had been working at the company for over thirty years, appeared agitated, perspiring, and flushed, as he retorted, "We have collectively decided that we won't work as long as you are our new leader. The current situation is unacceptable." In response, I calmly stated, "It is not your responsibility to determine whom the company employs or appoints to positions."

In response to my calm statement, he retorted, "Yes, I am aware of that. However, your presence as our leader is unacceptable, and we will fight until you leave this place. It's unacceptable for someone from Africa to be our leader." I recognized this remark as a racist comment, but I remained composed and collected. Leaving them to their discussion groups, I walked away. Suddenly, two Union representatives arrived at the department. They engaged in conversations with my "colleagues" and subsequently visited my office. They requested an opportunity to attempt resolving the issue with them. However, time was swiftly approaching the end of the workday.

Eventually, everyone left and went home, while I remained for over an hour, organizing papers and familiarizing myself with the logistics department's structure and job descriptions. I hoped that the following morning, these individuals would return and diligently carry out their duties. To my dismay, the next day, everyone arrived on time, grabbed their coffee cups, headed to the cafeteria or breakroom, and resumed their discussions, much like the previous day. The Union representatives arrived later, and the discussions continued, transforming into a sit-in protest against my leadership position. This unexpected and significant challenge caught me by surprise because these were individuals I considered my friends, aside from the two racist colleagues. Throughout our almost year-long tenure working together, we had fostered an environment of peace, harmony, and understanding. I never anticipated such a hostile reaction from them.

In addition to the ongoing tension, another part-time employee with underlying health problems began shouting derogatory remarks: "The last thing we will accept here is for an African to come and lead us as if we are stupid idiots." He persistently repeated these offensive comments until the Union representatives intervened, labelling it as a racist remark and declaring it unacceptable. By midday, only half of the workforce had resumed their duties, while the remaining employees remained angry and refused to work. Negotiations continued between the protesters and the Union, with the Union insisting that I give them time to try to persuade the protesters. Some individuals had already started contemplating a transfer to another department if the discussions did not go in their favour.

However, I understood that it would be challenging for anyone to leave such a desirable workplace for a less favourable alternative, hence several of them indicated not ready to move elsewhere after two or even three decades of working in the department. The duties and lower pay they would have in the factory were far less appealing. Another day passed, and the HR office had to become involved in the case, exploring options to relocate anyone wanting to leave their position to be relocated to the factory. During lunchtime at the canteen/restaurant, I attempted to maintain my composure and calm demeanour knowing that the rumour was going around. However, I couldn't help but worry about the possibility of my position being revoked and pondered what my course of action would be if such a scenario were to occur.

I also contemplated what kind of concessions could I come up with for the acceptance of my appointment by the seven remaining protestors. I came into the restaurant and found the place almost full on Friday afternoon. I took my lunch tray, fortunately saw an empty table and sat there. Just ten minutes later, our CEO came in, collected his food and came and sat with me. He asked, "How's it going with your new job?" I replied, "It's going great as I am quickly going through the files and reviewing the structures which might later require some changes for efficiency and effectiveness."

We both kept quiet for a minute or two, until he said again, "Are you sure everything is going fine at the department?" I responded, "Well, there are seven guys who insisted on not working since Monday due to my appointment." He then started narrating his own stories. He said he understood what was going on(as a disabled person), and he explained he had experienced great difficulties in life before becoming a top man. He emphasised repeatedly, that his life had been difficult but that I had to stand firm. He finally said, "Look, you have my backing, do what you think is right for you and the company—you have my full support, just let me know." I was full of confidence, self-assurance, and encouragement as we both left the canteen/restaurant and went back to our respective departments.

Coming back to the department, I grabbed a coffee and approached the group of disgruntled colleagues. Firmly, I addressed them, saying, "Today is the final day for anyone to come here and not meet the expectations of their work. I will be circulating a list for those who wish to continue the protest. I need it now, so I can take the necessary actions." With that, I returned to my office and instructed the secretary to create a list containing the names of those participating in the protest, along with a column for them to sign, indicating either 'Yes' or 'No,' along with a statement, "I declare that I will continue my sit-down protest next week." The list was typed up and circulated, making its way back to me by the end of the shift.

To my relief, the news was positive. All the names had ticked the 'No' column, signifying that they would not continue the protest. There was a sense of joy and laughter with my secretary as the rally concluded. Had they persisted, I had planned to relocate them out of the department and exert pressure on the HR office to swiftly find them alternative positions starting on Monday. While the department might face some short-term challenges, it would ultimately achieve peace and stability. Moreover, their reason for protesting was entirely unacceptable. One of my colleagues suggested filing a complaint against them for racism, but I opted against that route. Instead, I aimed to demonstrate maturity and wield my authority wisely to achieve cooperation. Perhaps, in due course, we would develop a better understanding and work together as a team to solve problems.

Over the weekend, I dedicated my time to the office, immersing myself in updating documents and analyzing figures. As Monday arrived, I felt rejuvenated, motivated, and optimistic about the department's prospects of operating at full capacity. And that's exactly what happened. Throughout the day, I primarily remained in my office, occasionally conducting general inspections to ensure everyone had the freedom to carry out their tasks. I made it clear that I was available to offer assistance if anyone encountered difficulties, emphasizing my role as part of the team, ready to help solve any problems that arose and maintain smooth operations. From Tuesday onwards, the department transformed. I encouraged the employees to seek advice or approach me whenever they faced challenges, fostering an atmosphere of openness and collaboration.

To demonstrate the new management's commitment, I initiated a series of improvements, including thorough cleaning, repainting, and providing new health and safety kits. The workplace was revitalized into a clean, vibrant, and inspiring environment that attracted everyone's attention. This transformation set the tone for the future. As the weeks passed without any friction or trouble, instead, it was marked by hard work and a spirit of teamwork. I had a close friend who owned a confectionery business located just five minutes away from our workplace. I reached out to him and negotiated the supply of freshly made cream cakes for the department every Friday afternoon. As a result, we all gathered in the meeting room, enjoying coffee and indulging in coffee and cream cake before wrapping up the week's work. The positive changes brought about a renewed sense of enthusiasm and camaraderie within the department.

As everyone revelled in their happiness, energy, and positive mood, I expressed my gratitude for their outstanding week of hard work and positivity, assuring them that this atmosphere would persist. I then made an exciting announcement, declaring that Friday coffee time with cream cake would become a cherished tradition, integrated into our new corporate department culture. This sparked enthusiastic conversations among the team. One of the team members remarked, "Why didn't we have something like this all these years, considering the effort we put into work?" In response, I simply assured them, "No problem, from now on, we'll have Friday coffee." The atmosphere was filled with lightheartedness and good humour, except for the two individuals who held prejudices against me.

However, I chose not to engage with their negativity. Instead, I allowed them to carry out their work freely, just as they always had. Once everyone had left and we began tidying up, one of the women approached me and commented, "You're a true professional. You genuinely want to make us happy, even those who don't like you." I replied, "It's not just about that. It's important to show appreciation and create a sense of togetherness. We have all worked hard toward the same goal, and it's wonderful to socialize, enjoy each other's company, and express our gratitude. I also believe in celebrating after putting in the effort." I emphasized the significance of motivating employees in various ways to foster a harmonious and engaging work environment. Treating everyone equally, exuding energy and focus while remaining calm, and being an attentive listener to all were key elements in my approach.

Recognizing the immense benefits of a motivated workforce, I prioritized creating a team that was dedicated, hardworking, and loyal. Achieving harmony, respect, and understanding among team members became crucial. To avoid any friction or conflicts within the team, I was clear about my expectations and took proactive steps to foster a positive work environment. Instead of engaging with those who harboured hatred towards me, I chose to focus on maintaining peace and harmony in the department. Moving them out would only disrupt productivity and hinder overall progress. Understanding that introducing new team members would require training and result in a temporary impact on productivity, I emphasized the importance of peace and harmony for smooth production flow. I considered this new position as a personal challenge and I was determined to excel. As time passed, week after week, the situation improved, and operations began to run seamlessly.

I made it a priority to be supportive to everyone on an equal basis. I ensured that no doubts lingered and that inquiries, questions, and concerns were addressed promptly and with the best possible answers. Every individual was made to feel equally important. Instead of giving orders and commands, I encouraged open dialogue by asking questions. I also made it a point to assign tasks according to each person's strengths and capabilities. Training opportunities were made accessible to those in need, as they benefitted both the individual and the company. After a couple of weeks of our enjoyable Friday coffee and cake sessions in the afternoon before leaving for the weekend, I decided to invite the CEO to join us. The CEO arrived while we were already seated, creating a welcoming atmosphere in our department. The time must have been around four in the afternoon.

He expressed gratitude for everyone's hard work and lightened the atmosphere with jokes and happily answered general questions from the team. The event was highly appreciated, and the CEO commended me for the initiative before we closed at five and headed into the weekend. While most weekends were dedicated to personal time, I occasionally came in on Saturdays to ensure I stayed updated on the SAP system, which was crucial for our department's operations. Meanwhile, the NGO and orphanage in Ghana continued to expand, despite the financial constraints. Fortunately, we were able to cover the expenses with the help of retired members who generously contributed their time and resources to the project. To focus more on my new full-time position, I delegated most of the NGO duties to committee members, trusting them to handle the day-to-day operations effectively.

On a particular weekend, I was selected, along with a few others from the Stockholm UN organization, by the Ministry of Foreign Affairs to participate in a working group. Our task was to develop recommendations on specific issues to be presented to the United Nations. As Sweden held a non-permanent seat at the Security Council, I was invited by the government to spend a weekend to provide a comprehensive working document. We dedicated ourselves to this task, working diligently at the foreign department ministry, and by Sunday night, we finalized the document. The topics addressed in our paper included extreme poverty and sustainability, as well as the pressing issues of deforestation and climate change.

The interconnectedness of these topics was paramount in our discussions and document, as we emphasized that solving one problem necessitates addressing the others. We condensed our recommendations into a small booklet, which would serve as a guide for the Swedish government's actions during their tenure at the Security Council over the next two years. Wealthy nations must develop relevant and effective solutions to support developing countries in their journey towards sustainability and combat deforestation. The level of poverty in developing countries, particularly in Africa, where a significant portion of the population lives on less than a dollar a day, is a complex and challenging issue to measure.

Having grown up in the Gambia, I witnessed a different form of poverty compared to what I saw in Sudan. While individuals like myself and many others had access to three meals a day, decent schools, and a living standard that might be considered sub-standard in the West but acceptable by African standards, the situation in Sudan and other places are more dire. In regions like Darfur and Kordofan, severe droughts forced women to embark on days-long journeys with donkeys or camels in search of water. Sudan has a substantial nomadic society, where people migrate with herd animals from one place to another in search of green places. The realities of poverty differ across regions and countries, highlighting the need for tailored approaches that address specific challenges faced by different communities. Understanding these nuances is crucial in formulating effective strategies and interventions to alleviate poverty and promote sustainable development.

In the outskirts of town, within refugee camps where our collaborative efforts with the government, UNICEF, and UNHCR were focused, a distressing reality unfolded. Each day, an alarming number of children succumbed to malnutrition and other related ailments. This level of poverty is profoundly distressing in this 21st century. It is unjust that these individuals, struggling to survive, are unable to prioritize environmental conservation while grappling with the fundamental challenge of hunger. Addressing extreme poverty and allocating resources to these marginalized communities would not only alleviate their suffering but also empower them to protect and preserve our forests.

During this period, my relationship with Sana remained stable albeit with occasional bumps along the way. Numerous surveys conducted in Sweden reveal that relationships often falter not primarily due to financial issues but as a result of an unfair distribution of domestic responsibilities, such as dishwashing, laundry, cleaning, and cooking, which still predominantly burden women. Our relationship mirrored this pattern, leading us to engage in debates over the allocation of household chores. I find satisfaction in taking care of all domestic tasks and maintaining an organized living environment, which Sana often did not prioritize. When she was at work and I was at home, I assumed the responsibility of handling nearly everything around the house. I believed that the same principle should apply to her, expecting her to take on her fair share of household duties.

There were instances when I would return home, hoping that dinner would be prepared, only to find that Sana was waiting for me to cook. Whenever I expressed my concern, her response was consistent, "But you're the best cook." Over the years, she never displayed an interest in learning to cook. When she travelled for work, it was easier for me as I could always keep some food for the next day. However, whenever she was around, I couldn't rely on having leftovers. There were occasions when I cooked an ample amount, intending to save some for later since we were both busy. Unfortunately, she would end up consuming everything, leaving me exhausted and late to prepare another meal. This became one of the major issues in our marriage, particularly when I wanted to avoid relying too heavily on fast food.

However, cooking wasn't the only challenge we faced; there was also a breakdown in maintaining tidiness and order around the house. After discussing these matters with her for years, I reached a point where I no longer found it amusing for a husband to constantly pick up scattered underwear and socks throughout the house. I couldn't simply overlook these things, especially when she brushed them off with jokes and exhibited no willingness to change. Finally, one day, I suggested that we consider separation as a means to potentially shift her attitude. Almost immediately, I regretted uttering those words. She spent the entire day in tears, expressing that she would take her life if we were to separate or divorce. Her distress was so overwhelming, her cries echoing throughout the house, that I couldn't bear to ignore or handle it alone. I worried that our neighbours might hear her anguish.

Within a matter of weeks, I broached the topic again, but this time her reaction was one of outrage. She exclaimed, "We never quarrel, never argue. We have no financial problems, and I believe our relationship is perfect." I responded by saying, "Well, there are certain things we need to address and assist each other with. You need to be supportive and take responsibility around the house. It's no longer amusing when I come home late and have to start cooking while you've been at home all day doing nothing." Despite the challenges, I persisted in expressing my concerns. I continued, "If we truly want to have a great, fair, and loving relationship, we must show empathy and care for each other. We need to listen to each other's concerns. Otherwise, if you're unwilling to listen, I will conclude that you don't value the relationship but only yourself."

Understanding and recognizing that a relationship is a two-way street, where both individuals strive to satisfy each other's needs, is crucial. Despite emphasizing the need for separation, I assured her that I still loved her. I hoped that my constant insistence would prevent any irreversible actions. However, as long as she remained resistant to change, I found myself becoming increasingly prepared to let the relationship come to an end. One of her closest friends, also of Russian origin, was aware of our problems. She visited us and cheerfully remarked, "How can you let go of such a beautiful girl that no other man would refuse? She's someone any man would dream of having."

For me, it wasn't solely about her physical beauty but rather the quality of her personality and how it impacted our relationship, enabling us to live harmoniously and meaningfully together. The unbalanced distribution of responsibilities in the household, where I constantly fulfilled my obligations while she did nothing, felt unfair. Just as I would not have wanted all the household chores to fall solely on her shoulders, I expected a more equitable arrangement. As time went on, I grew increasingly weary of the situation and did not wish for it to continue. There were moments when she seemed to take my concerns for granted, making light of them and assuming that I could never leave her. She continued making comments half-jokingly, about taking her own life, perhaps aware of my compassionate nature.

Despite her comments, I knew deep down that it was not a genuine threat and that she would never harm herself if we were to separate. I reminded her, "With the wealth you have accumulated and the numerous friends you have, why would you consider ending your life over one man, namely me? Think of all the other wonderful things life has to offer." On one occasion, she even offered to give me all of her money, as if that were the source of the problem. However, it had nothing to do with finances, as we both earned enough and had no outstanding debts apart from the usual expenses such as rent, electricity, water, and internet bills. I covered the monthly rent through direct debit from my account, while she paid a portion of the electricity and internet bills, which amounted to less than my share.

However, the issue of money had no relevance to our underlying problems. It wasn't about who would buy what or who would pay for what. There were moments when I almost reconsidered my decision to leave her, feeling sorry for her difficult days when she would spend the entire day in bed, filled with regret. However, I knew that if we were to separate, I needed to remain consistent, or else it would never happen. I stuck to my decision, hoping that eventually, we could reach a consensus. After nearly six months of discussions and attempts to convince her to separate, I finally gathered her belongings and assisted her in moving to her friend's place upon returning from a trip to Paris.

It was a sombre moment, but after investing considerable time in trying to change the situation, it became clear that she had little inclination to put in the effort required to make things work. Thus, living separately seemed to be the only viable option. The separation would serve as a trial period, during which we would engage in serious discussions and make promises before considering reconciliation. She underestimated my resolve, assuming that I would miss her so intensely that I would quickly change my mind and chase after her. I suspect this might have been a plan orchestrated by her friend. As a few months passed, consumed with work and other matters, I didn't hear much from her. She distanced herself, which contrasted with the initial weeks after moving out when she would call me multiple times a day until bedtime, teasingly asking, "Did you miss me, Zaya?" Zaya is the Russian word for Bunny, which was her nickname for me.

She called me after almost two months, sharing that she was in China after being invited by the Managing Director of a Swedish multinational corporation based there. I felt genuinely happy for her, as it seemed like a new direction was unfolding in her life. I expressed, "I think you should consider marrying him, and we can continue to be good friends." She abruptly ended the call, and I didn't hear from her again until two days later. During that conversation, I mentioned that I could contact the registry office to initiate the divorce process. I assured her, "You have the keys to the house, and you're always welcome. You don't even need to call before coming." After a couple of weeks, she informed me that her new friend had purchased a spacious two-room apartment in the centre of Stockholm for her.

I felt a sense of relief, not because of the apartment itself, but because she was gradually detaching from me. However, she continued to call and share every detail about what her new friend told her or suggested, who proposed marriage to her. Years later, I came across an interview she gave on Radio Stockholm P1 during a summer talk show where she was the guest. She mentioned that she had always desired a long-lasting marriage and had made attempts in the past but never succeeded in finding a relationship where she could plan for a family. I couldn't help but wonder how honest she was in that interview, considering the numerous opportunities I had given her to achieve a stable and lasting relationship. Nevertheless, I insisted on not keeping the keys to her new apartment, as she had proposed.

Karin was saddened by the situation but maintained close contact with me, as did the rest of our family. I shifted my focus more towards my work and other important activities. I engaged in weekend UN conferences and workshops, and I even started participating in running again, intending to run marathons. My commitment to my professional role at work became increasingly significant to me. While there was harmony within my department, I encountered further challenges, primarily from leaders outside of my team, such as supervisors, engineers, and external contractors. I noticed their attempts to assign blame to me for any faults even those unknown, which I understand to be trying to undermine my position.

In response, I became extremely cautious and focused. I made sure to document most actions in writing, paying close attention to timing and content. The habit of documenting things over time became an important management tool for me. I also delegated tasks to those who were best suited while also empowering them with responsibilities. I ensured that I didn't get involved in anything I don't fully understand. I took no chances when it came to attracting blame that could endanger my position. I sought clarification on anything I had limited understanding of, avoiding assumptions or misunderstandings.

The department I worked in consisted of highly experienced colleagues who had been performing the same work for decades. While their expertise was valuable, an important aspect of management is problem-solving and prevention. My daily objective was to ensure stable production throughout the entire department. To achieve this, I carefully assessed everyone's competencies and positioned them in roles which best suited them. To maintain focus and productivity, I implemented measures to prevent distractions during work. I made it clear that all external individuals seeking to approach me would have to go through the secretary first. I refused to be easily disturbed or diverted, particularly by what I referred to as "time-wasters." I wanted to shield myself from any news or discussions that would hinder my concentration on work.

I consistently approached my work with a serious and dedicated mindset. As time passed, I noticed a positive shift in the department. The collaborative spirit grew, and everyone became more dedicated to their tasks. The two individuals who held animosity towards me, openly expressing their racist views, began to falter in performing their assigned responsibilities. Their actions mostly consisted of nagging, chatting, and disrupting others from carrying out their work effectively. I was aware that they continued to express their refusal to accept me as their leader, but I chose not to react to such rumours, considering them beneath my attention. It was all part of my strategy to avoid conflicts or any distractions that could hinder productivity.

The end of each month was always a challenging period for the entire department. My monthly goals revolved around two key points: ensuring the smooth functioning of the entire supply chain system and achieving sales growth. Additionally, managing the workforce and ensuring their motivation and optimal performance were also priorities. The last Friday of every month was dedicated to focused and hard work, with a strong emphasis on meeting period targets. We successfully and steadily increased our sales, which was reflected in the quarterly reports and figures. The department's achievements were celebrated, acknowledging the collective efforts of the team.

Additionally, there was a half-yearly inventory activity conducted in collaboration with the central office to account for all goods in the warehouse. Maintaining a strong network of contacts was crucial for my role. I regularly interacted with the sales and marketing department, production department, economy department, and municipal workers. External contractors were also held accountable for adhering to health and safety guidelines and any agreements established between them and the company. I consistently aimed to minimize waste and implement effective management systems within the department. An "ideas box" was available for everyone in the department, and I took this initiative seriously. During our Friday coffee breaks, we would review the submitted ideas and collectively determine which ones were relevant and feasible to implement.

During that time, I often generated ideas that saved the company significant amounts of money in the short, medium, and long term. However, I intentionally refrained from seeking compensation for these ideas to prevent any rumours of self-reward. I maintained a cautious approach, ensuring that my actions did not give rise to controversy or speculation. This was one of the reasons why I adopted an open-door policy, allowing for transparent communication and feedback. Nevertheless, individuals who contributed valuable ideas or made the systems more efficient were appropriately recognized and rewarded.

There was an incident involving one of the individuals who held a dislike towards me. He proposed an idea that was deemed impractical by both myself and others in the department. It involved placing a small table in each toilet room for people to write down ideas. I explained to him the logistical challenges and questioned the feasibility of spending time in the toilet writing down ideas while others were busy working. He became angry and distanced himself for a few days.

On another normal Monday morning, I noticed a car parked in the area typically designated for trucks waiting for their loads. This was unusual, as I had driven past the area earlier in the morning and the car was not there. I inquired about the car and one of my colleagues volunteered to check if someone was inside and why it'd been parked there. It was evident that someone was indeed in the car. After a few minutes, the colleague returned to the office, visibly out of breath after a snap run.

The discovery of a deceased person in the car parked outside was a shocking and tragic incident. I immediately instructed everyone not to touch anything and advised them to wait for the police to arrive as it was a crime scene. The secretary promptly contacted the nearby police station, which was just a minute away on the same street. Later, I documented the incident by writing a short incident report. Unfortunately, news of the incident spread rapidly throughout the company, fuelled by human curiosity. It was a sombre and unsettling event that had a significant impact on the workplace atmosphere.

On alternating Fridays, the CEO would visit my department to discuss ongoing projects, particularly related to the substantial investments being made by the US Mum company. These investments included the implementation of new machinery and the introduction of new product lines. During these meetings, we also focused on the benefits of the new flat organizational structure, which aimed to quickly and effectively address problems, motivate employees, foster a sense of ownership and responsibility, and ensure inclusivity throughout the decision-making process. To assess progress, a management consulting company conducted biannual evaluations to measure employee satisfaction, the distribution of responsibilities, and overall motivation levels.

Fortunately, significant advancements were observed in each assessment. Leading a contemporary workforce differs greatly from ancient times when individuals lacked rights and education. The conventional approach of issuing commands devoid of gratitude or displaying disinterest, apathy, or lack of empathy towards employees is met with disapproval by many. An effective leader ensures that employees are not merely motivated by their paycheck but rather possess genuine passion and enthusiasm for their work, while also being granted the autonomy to operate without constant supervision. Excessive micromanagement hinders the cultivation of a creative, innovative, and impassioned team.

It can be tiring for a leader to scrutinize every minute detail, whether it's for rectification or providing feedback. Sometimes, it is beneficial to overlook certain matters and refrain from constant monitoring. The best way to learn from mistakes is to allow individuals to self-correct. Micromanagement proves to be less effective as it undermines self-confidence and stifles creativity. As I embarked on living independently, I wholeheartedly dedicated myself to my job and strived for peak performance each day. I ensured the availability of all necessary tools and materials to facilitate an uninterrupted flow within the entire supply chain system. However, I never grew complacent and never took anything for granted.

Under my leadership, the department experienced remarkable growth, particularly in terms of cost savings, operational efficiency, and the establishment of an effective waste management system. The entire team actively participated and consistently strived for improved outcomes at the end of each reporting period. At one point, I conceived an idea to revamp the shelving system, which, based on my calculations, had the potential to save millions of krona and significantly reduce loading time. Additionally, it would greatly benefit the drivers collecting these goods. The implementation of this idea promised advantages for all stakeholders. To ensure clarity and coherence, I meticulously documented the comprehensive plan for the proposed changes in a straightforward and informative manner. Initially, I shared the concept with the secretary, who responded with enthusiasm and optimism.

However, she anticipated that some workers might oppose the idea, necessitating negotiations to garner their support. The plan remained confidential until one Friday afternoon during our coffee session when I made the announcement. I estimated that it would take approximately three Saturdays to fully implement the idea. However, before proceeding, I sought the team's feedback on the project. As anticipated, four individuals voiced their opposition without providing substantial reasons. One team member expressed, "I have been working here for nearly thirty years, and we have always followed the same process, which has worked well. Now you want to introduce these unnecessary changes." In response, I explained, "I intend to enhance the overall experience for everyone, as it falls within my responsibility to strive for improvement."

The involvement of relevant stakeholders, particularly those directly impacted, is crucial for the successful implementation of any change or reform initiative. It is essential to engage individuals from the outset of the project and maintain their active participation throughout the entire process, including the implementation and closing phases. This approach holds significant importance in project work. By involving people, we not only instil a sense of pride and ownership but also ensure that the benefits of success are shared equally. Furthermore, incorporating individuals into the project fosters better understanding among workers, which is a fundamental element for establishing a stable and harmonized workplace that delivers excellent results.

As I explained, "The purpose of these proposed changes is to enhance the well-being of everyone involved and create a more beneficial outcome." I elaborated on the details, emphasizing that the waiting time would be eliminated, thus clearing the backlog and enhancing our overall performance. However, the response I received was disheartening: "No, we do not welcome any changes. We will bring this matter to the Union." It seemed like a dead-end. Despite asking for questions or alternative ideas to move forward with the changes, everyone remained silent. These proposed changes, if implemented, would result in significant time savings and increased revenue. Determined to proceed with the project despite the opposition,

I compiled a detailed plan in a presentation document. I included a graph illustrating the number of hours we would save weekly, monthly and annually, then explained how it would improve the effectiveness of the entire value chain while also addressing the backlog. A week later, a meeting commenced with the presence of all team members, accompanied by a spread of coffee and doughnuts. The project presentation was displayed, and ready for discussion. Surprisingly, the individual who vehemently opposed any changes just a week and a half ago had a change of heart. He announced that he no longer objected and was now open to accepting any proposed changes. I took the opportunity to remind them, saying, "Some of you have frequently expressed dissatisfaction with the drivers waiting for hours and utilizing the facilities, especially the canteen."

Now, I had three remaining individuals to persuade, one of whom had initially displayed dislike towards me from the first day we met. Regardless of what I said or did, they seemed determined to oppose anything that came from me. During our earlier discussions, they had threatened to involve the Union if I insisted on proceeding with the project. I was not overly concerned about the Union's involvement since the project aimed to improve the system and benefit everyone. Additionally, the fact that the majority of team members supported the initiative would strengthen my position in case the Union decided to escalate the matter. Following that meeting, I began collecting the names of those interested in participating in the project, to commence the following weekend on Saturday.

When the secretary presented the list to my two adversaries and inquired if they wanted to be involved, they responded with a firm, "No." However, they acknowledged that the project could proceed without their participation and stated that they would not interfere or disrupt its progress. They took the opportunity to express their belief that everything I initiated would ultimately lead to disaster for the department. Although their comments didn't deter me, I made it clear that what I needed for the project to commence was the dedication and active participation of those involved. During the project timeline, the CEO paid a visit accompanied by guests from the USA. We engaged in conversation, touching upon topics such as my experience living in the USA in the 1980s, sales numbers, work-related challenges, and the progress we had made so far.

We also discussed the upcoming project and its potential to enhance production, drive increased sales, and generate higher revenue once implemented. I further elaborated on the project's objectives, which included reducing delivery time, minimizing the waiting time for drivers, increasing the overall supply, boosting revenue, and eliminating the backlog that had persisted for years, thus resolving customer complaints. In response, our CEO chuckled and remarked, "Let's examine the figures later and keep our fingers crossed." We initiated the project on Saturday morning and concluded it after three weeks. At the end of the endeavour, I expressed my gratitude and appreciation to everyone involved for their invaluable contributions to the project's success.

Following the completion of the project, I decided to send a special 'Thank You' card to everyone's home address as an extra gesture of appreciation. I wanted to ensure that expressing gratitude went beyond a mere verbal acknowledgement in front of everyone. I believed that personalizing the gesture would make it more meaningful. Only a week passed after the project's conclusion when we began witnessing remarkable changes in the figures as I updated the numbers on the whiteboard. Collection times were drastically reduced, providing us with more time to address the backlog of orders that had accumulated over a considerable period. As the figures emerged the following week, the entire office started buzzing with discussions about our impressive progress. The credit truly belonged to everyone, especially those who sacrificed their family time on three consecutive Saturdays to be part of this achievement. It was a remarkable outcome resulting from the collective effort of the team.

Surprisingly, one of the individuals who had expressed his hateful views towards me and immigrants, particularly towards black people, over a year ago, suddenly started addressing me as "Boss" out of the blue. This unexpected change occurred one morning at the coffee machine. Initially, I ignored him, grabbed my coffee, and made my way to my office, which was only about fifteen metres away. Curious about this sudden shift, I called my secretary and asked her if I had imagined the whole interaction. "It was an unexpectedly pleasant morning," she replied, "and it could be interpreted as a sign that he was easing up and perhaps feeling remorse for his past aggression and animosity towards you." Despite this change, I continued to maintain professionalism in my interactions with him, ensuring that he adhered to his job responsibilities and followed the company's rules and regulations. As long as we could all work peacefully as a team, I believed in approaching the situation with maturity.

Despite the awkwardness of the situation with the individual who now referred to me as "Boss," I chose to respond with a smile and inquire if everything was right whenever we crossed paths. I would then quickly shift my focus to other tasks. The word 'Boss' echoed in my ears each time, but only in those moments when we were alone. In such situations, I maintained my belief in tolerance, patience, and resilience, remaining determined and assertive when necessary while prioritizing the well-being of the workers alongside the company's objectives. I understood that time often serves as the best healer, and as time passed, I sensed that the animosity surrounding me was gradually dissipating in practice. Nevertheless, there were certain aspects beyond my control, and in such cases, it was best to let go.

On a different note, an external electrician contractor contacted me to discuss a job at the department. We had a cordial conversation over the phone, and I gave him time to visit the office. When he arrived, he asked for me by name. I went out to greet him, and upon seeing me, he turned his back towards my secretary, who was already leaving, and exclaimed loudly, "I said I am asking for the boss I spoke with earlier today." My secretary responded firmly, "That's him standing in front of you. What else do you want?" I intervened, saying, "We did speak earlier, and I instructed you to come in." However, he persisted and insisted, "No, but can I speak with your boss?" Recognizing the futility of the situation, I replied, "Alright," and left him there as I returned to my office.

Upon being redirected to my office again, the external electrician proceeded to the logistics office and requested to speak with the section boss, only to be sent back to me once more. It was evident that he hadn't expected to encounter a black man in the position of a section boss. He quickly apologized, expressing his unawareness of our previous conversation. I guided him to the designated work area, reviewed his work papers and plans, and then emphasized the importance of complying with company rules, particularly regarding health and safety, as I handed him the relevant documents. Instances of such attitudes are beyond my control, and I chose to let them go, recognizing that I cannot alter people's inherent biases or prejudices towards me.

My secretary commented that our former manager, despite being German and having worked here for over twenty years, had never encountered such behaviour. I responded by saying, "Yes, remember that I am different from a German."

Understanding the implication, she grasped my point. Coinciding with the company's acquisition by an American firm, the official corporate currency transitioned to the dollar, and English became the designated corporate language. This change came at an opportune time for me. I was the only one in the entire department who was fluent in English, while others could only communicate in simple sentences and words without proficiency in the language. English became a valuable tool for me in managing certain aspects of the department's affairs, particularly in my correspondence with the economics department.

I successfully implemented various aspects of corporate culture, values, vision, and mission statements within the department. This involved translating them into Swedish, displaying them on our information board, and engaging in discussions to ensure that our daily activities and responsibilities were in line with the company's objectives and ambitions.

In the western part of Sweden, Gothenburg, we encountered a persistent customer complaint regarding the non-receipt of goods. To address this issue, we promptly sent a replacement order, considering the initial shipment as lost. Interestingly, this particular customer was the only one consistently reporting such incidents, despite us serving a large number of customers, without any similar complaints.

Growing increasingly frustrated, I decided to delve deeper into the matter of these alleged lost goods. To my surprise, everyone in the office unanimously concluded that this customer had been intentionally receiving the initial consignments and then falsely claiming non-receipt to obtain additional shipments. Interestingly, this customer happened to be the same individual who previously held a managerial position and had made my life difficult during my tenure as a production team leader, exhibiting behaviour that could be considered bullying. Initially, I had contemplated assigning the regional salesperson to handle this customer's case. Although this salesperson never addressed me directly, they were always willing to carry out the tasks I assigned. However, I changed my mind and decided to personally visit the customer, keeping it a surprise for them.

Armed with a list of EAN numbers, which are unique identifiers for product barcodes, I embarked on a five-and-a-half-hour journey to meet the customer. My objective was to investigate the reported non-receipt of items from the previous consignment. Having only spoken over the phone, the customer had never met me before. Upon entering his shop, I wasted no time and immediately began comparing the EAN numbers on my list with the products on the shelves. To ensure optimal product placement, we had previously agreed with customers to position items prominently, often near the cashier or along the queue leading to the cashier. As customers went about their shopping, I discreetly pulled out my list from my briefcase and meticulously cross-referenced the product numbers. Astonishingly, the products he had claimed never to have received were right there on the shelves.

At that moment, the customer was attending to another shopper at the cash counter. Once he finished, he approached me and inquired about my identity. I introduced myself, mentioning my name and the company I represented. To my surprise, he responded with a mixture of joy and laughter upon recognizing my voice. He exclaimed, "Oh, I never thought you were a black man, even after speaking with you several times." However, it's worth noting that he had previously informed me that he hailed from Iran. Without dwelling on his comment, I swiftly redirected the conversation to the matter at hand, emphasizing its importance.

I presented before him the list of products he had claimed not to have received, which I now found prominently displayed on his shelves. Overwhelmed with surprise, he was left speechless and embarrassed. Seizing the opportunity, I took photographs of the products and sternly reminded him of the potential legal consequences his actions could entail. I emphasized that the company had the right to take him to court, demanding full reimbursement for every single penny owed. I urged him to reflect upon the numerous instances he had contacted us, sounded frustrated and falsely reported lost goods and subsequently received replacement shipments. Caught off guard, he began to stammer, expressing remorse and guilt for his actions. He inquired anxiously whether the company intended to pursue legal action against him. I assured him that I would consult with my colleagues and bosses to decide in the coming days.

Overwhelmed by the gravity of the situation, he stressed that he would never engage in such behaviour again. He even proposed a settlement wherein he would willingly pay a specific amount to settle the matter without involving the police. We stood there for another twenty minutes as he expressed his deep remorse. Eventually, I resolved with him. I drafted a declaration outlining the details of his cheating, supported by the evidence I had gathered (the photos and the list of products). In exchange for his signature, he agreed that if he ever complained about non-delivery again, the evidence would be handed over to the police. With a sense of relief, he happily signed the dated document and pledged to become our most exemplary customer.

I responded, "Well, considering we have thousands of customers, and you are the only one who consistently reports non-receipt of goods, it certainly raises some questions. We are fortunate to have many wonderful customers who uphold good moral values and would never resort to such dishonest practices." Upon returning to work on Monday, I shared the story of my encounter with this customer, highlighting the positive outcome. It became an engaging and uplifting tale within the office. From that point on, the customer ceased calling about lost consignments and continued as a regular, reliable customer. Maintaining a high level of organization has always been one of my strengths. I have consistently relied on my to-do list, which assists me in remembering important tasks, locating necessary items, and ensuring that actions are taken at the appropriate time.

Throughout my life, colleagues have often commented on my exceptional organizational skills. I find it frustrating when others display a lack of organization, such as arriving late to meetings, forgetting important details, or struggling to locate essential documents. Therefore, I place great importance on effective time management. Being well-organized not only contributes to personal credibility but also serves as a valuable tool for leadership and management roles. It is often said that the state of a leader's desk reflects their level of organization. I have always been highly motivated to learn new things. The desire for continuous learning is ingrained in my nature, and it fuels my personal and professional growth.

I always seek out challenges in life as they keep things interesting and prevent monotony from setting in. One Friday evening after work, when darkness had already descended, some of the ladies in the office and a few others suggested going to the bar/restaurant located inside the mall. Initially, I declined the invitation, but as more voices joined in, I was eventually persuaded to join them. Reluctantly, I consented, and we all made our way to the bar/restaurant. Upon arrival, we found a table in the central area. The place was moderately crowded, with people enjoying their drinks and a few individuals on the dance floor. We placed our drink orders, and I opted for my usual orange beverage. Engaging in conversations and relishing the company of my colleagues, we settled into the evening.

Not long after, a stunning young lady wearing a flowing white dress approached our table and extended an invitation for me to dance. Politely, I declined, explaining that we had just come from work and I wasn't in the mood for dancing. She lingered nearby, patiently awaiting the completion of my sentence. After approximately fifteen minutes, she returned and implored me once again to join her on the dance floor. Realizing that my previous response hadn't dissuaded her, I reiterated, "As I mentioned before, I truly don't feel like dancing tonight. Coming here was something I didn't want to do in the first place." With that, she left once more. At our table, everyone shared a laugh, and some suggested that I should have danced with her for just a few minutes. Little did they know what was about to happen. To everyone's surprise, she made her way back for the third time.

This time, it was met with even more laughter and amusement. In a lighthearted spirit, I decided to follow her to the dance floor and indulge in dance, embracing the unexpected twist of the evening.

As the music filled the air, a few couples swayed on the dance floor. Once we began dancing, the lady held me tightly, wrapping her arms around my neck. I couldn't help but wonder if she had been drinking, but there was no scent of alcohol indicating otherwise. We continued to dance in that intimate position, moving slowly as if we were a couple. I eagerly awaited the end of the song. Suddenly, I felt a tap on my shoulder. The lady, unaware of the interruption, had nestled her head comfortably on my other shoulder. I turned my head to see a man standing nearby. He spoke, "This is my wife. We just got married a couple of hours ago, and we're here to celebrate." Instantly, I withdrew, realizing what was going on. The lady stepped back, appearing angry with her husband.

They began arguing loudly, and I swiftly made my way back to the table. The incident sparked a wave of laughter among my colleagues, who jokingly remarked that I had unintentionally tried to claim someone else's wife. However, such occurrences were not uncommon in Sweden. It is a society where individuals, especially women, have the freedom to express themselves and their feelings openly, without it being seen as a significant issue. People exercise their freedom and liberty to express emotions outside of marriage without it being overly scrutinized. Despite the unexpected encounter, we continued to enjoy ourselves for the remainder of the evening. Laughter and lightheartedness prevailed, and we eventually left the venue around midnight, concluding a memorable and eventful night.

About four weeks later, on another Friday after work, the same group from the office suggested returning to the same restaurant for dinner, and I thought it was a fantastic idea. As evening fell, around 6 p.m., we made our way to the restaurant, it was already engulfed in darkness. Once again, we occupied the familiar table and proceeded to place our orders, knowing that the restaurant consistently served delicious Turkish cuisine, and the owner was a good friend of mine. The atmosphere was relaxed as we began to eat and engage in lively conversations. Seated directly across from me was my secretary. Suddenly, she extended her arm over my head and delivered a swift slap to someone standing behind me. Bewildered, I realized that an individual had been pouring beer onto my hat without my knowledge. The liquid had trickled down my hat and onto my shoulders, drenching them.

My secretary continued to confront the person, repeatedly slapping him, leaving me stunned by the unexpected turn of events transpiring above my head. Others at the table also rose to their feet, ready to confront the offender who was still standing behind me. Confused, I inquired, "What's happening?" In response, my secretary exclaimed, "He was pouring beer on your hat!" It was then that I stood up and felt the dampness on my right shoulder and back, accompanied by the distinct smell of beer emanating from my hat. Security personnel swiftly intervened, escorting the individual out of the establishment. We later discovered him standing outside, persistently attempting to re-enter despite the efforts of the security guard. That incident marked the end of my visits to that particular restaurant, as the memory of that event lingered.

Once, we encountered an outage caused by an incident at a railway station approximately one kilometre away from our location of work. The power failure affected our operations, and unfortunately, the standby generator that was supposed to kick in during such situations failed to function. It was revealed that the generator had never been tested by the section engineers as it should have been done monthly. This realization left us without any work production or deliveries for the day, including the main office. Transports arrived and departed without being loaded. This incident prompted me to devise a contingency system to ensure we could still supply our most crucial customers in the event of a future outage.

Contingency planning is a vital aspect of effective management systems as it allows for addressing potential problems or emergencies, minimizing or even preventing the loss of productivity and revenue. Given the ample space available in our warehouse, I conceived the idea of setting up a manual contingency system where the supply chain could be managed manually. I identified an empty area where the project could be implemented and introduced the idea to our team. Despite initial scepticism, the idea was embraced by everyone, although doubts remained regarding whether the Finance department would support and approve it. Nevertheless, I remained determined to pursue it. Within a week of conceptualizing the idea, I enlisted the help of my secretary to conduct an environmental study to support the feasibility and implementation of the contingency system. Together, we set out to gather the necessary information to present a well-researched and compelling case.

A comprehensive cost analysis was conducted, accompanied by a concise description outlining the benefits and advantages of implementing a manual contingency supply chain system. The project plan, prepared in English, was then submitted to the Finance department for their review and consideration. Following brief discussions with the department and the Union, we eagerly awaited their response, all while harbouring concerns that the proposal might face rejection due to funding constraints. After three weeks, I received an invitation from the Finance department to discuss the project further. I decided to bring my secretary along for the meeting. However, deep down, I held a sceptical belief that the proposal would likely be met with negative news, citing budget limitations and financial constraints.

Upon our arrival at the Finance office, we stopped by the kitchen to grab some coffee before proceeding to the meeting room. Coincidentally, we encountered a familiar colleague who was known for her sense of humour. She approached us and whispered, "It's going to be good news, don't worry." We exchanged glances, smiled, laughed, and continued to the meeting room with newfound optimism. The meeting itself proceeded smoothly and efficiently. After addressing a few questions, the project was recognized for its merit, and the availability of financing was confirmed and officially approved. Subsequently, we reached out to several private companies, and the contract was awarded to the most suitable bidder. During the project's progress, our CEO paid a visit and jokingly remarked, "I can see you're doing well, maybe even better than I am. Perhaps we should swap positions!"

After successfully implementing the project, I began to notice a shift in how I was perceived by my colleagues. It became apparent when I experienced a couple of instances where my car was unexpectedly cleared of snow during winter evenings when I had stayed late at work. I couldn't help but wonder who was performing this thoughtful act. As it happened again, I confided in my secretary about my curiosity regarding the person responsible for clearing the snow from my car. The following day, my secretary approached me with an answer. She revealed that it was the very same individual who had openly expressed his disdain towards me due to his racist beliefs. I was taken aback and asked her how she came to know this information. She explained that he had shared it with her the day before, and she had informed him of my curiosity about the kind-hearted person behind the act.

I found it astonishing how people can transform their behaviour over time. This individual, who once harboured deep animosity towards me, now went out of his way to address me as "Boss" and take care of my car, perhaps seeking recognition or approval from me. During our performance appraisal meetings, he even expressed a desire to participate in various courses and self-development programmes. Our workplace offered a range of courses covering topics such as fire safety, food and hygiene, alcoholism awareness, environmental driving, first aid, and Samaritan training etc. Additionally, the Union provided free courses for members on personal finance, workers' rights, retirement planning, and many other subjects. It was encouraging to witness this transformation in my colleague, as he displayed a genuine willingness to grow and improve. It served as a reminder that people can change their perspectives and behaviours and that providing opportunities for personal development can have a positive impact on individuals and the overall work environment.

Supporting subordinates in achieving their goals and fostering their growth is crucial for effective leadership. Empowering employees to develop themselves instils optimism and drives them to embrace responsibility and take ownership of their tasks. A highly skilled workforce not only excels but also yields superior outcomes. To illustrate, I took proactive measures to assist a worker struggling with alcohol addiction. Recognizing the impact of this issue on his performance, I facilitated his enrolment in a week-long alcohol de-addiction course. The course proved immensely beneficial, as he successfully overcame his drinking problem within six months. Previously, he had arrived at work intoxicated on a few occasions, necessitating his early dismissal. I facilitated his participation in the course and provided ongoing support to all interested individuals.

My dedication extended beyond work responsibilities. I prioritized the well-being of my colleagues, striving to give my best every day. Simultaneously, I managed to allocate time for my involvement in NGO initiatives, occasional rounds of golf on Sundays, and efficient daily planning to ensure a balanced schedule. Additionally, I continued expanding my knowledge by avidly reading literature on management and leadership. During an appraisal meeting with a co-worker who harboured racist beliefs, the conversation took an unexpected turn. As soon as we sat down, he began showering me with unwarranted praise, commending my performance beyond his expectations. However, I promptly redirected the focus of the meeting, urging him to refrain from such praise, as it deviated from its intended purpose

During one appraisal session with one of my subordinates, I inquired about his comments and aspirations for self-advancement in the upcoming year. To my surprise, he responded by asking what he needed to do to lead the department. Clarifying his intention, I asked if he meant my position, to which he affirmed. In response, I candidly stated that he would first have to modify his behaviour. The room fell into complete silence, and at that moment, the secretary entered, taking over the discussion while I attended to other matters. In my view, discipline and composure are indispensable qualities for effective leadership. Demonstrating respect for all employees, refraining from the abuse of power, and treating everyone fairly and compassionately is of utmost importance. As someone responsible for establishing rules and regulations, I hold a deep appreciation for law and order and steadfastly uphold them. Leading by example is paramount, as it encourages others to embrace the principles and culture set forth by the organization.

It is worth noting that leaders are constantly under observation, even when they may not be aware of it. Others keenly observe their actions, communication skills, and relationships with personnel. Unfair treatment, manipulation, and a tendency to deviate from the truth undermine both credibility and authority, ultimately leading to chaos and disorder. In this 21st century, leaders must exhibit compassion, emotional intelligence, and a humanistic approach. These qualities are essential for effective leadership. By embodying these attributes, leaders can earn respect, inspire motivation, and foster dedication in their workforce. When employees recognize these qualities in their leader, a greater sense of respect, loyalty and authority is cultivated.

When a leader exemplifies strong performance and takes their duties and responsibilities seriously, it sets a positive tone that permeates throughout the organization, fostering high levels of productivity and maintaining law and order. The leader catalyzes the team's success, and their actions have a ripple effect. One key aspect is cultivating openness and creating an environment where people feel comfortable expressing divergent opinions. Embracing tolerance nurtures effective teamwork, ultimately leading to heightened productivity. Striking a balance between maintaining self-respect and being open to others' perspectives is crucial. Engaging in meaningful conversations, wearing a genuine smile, displaying a sincere interest in people, and actively listening all contribute to fostering a positive atmosphere. The leader should also demonstrate decisiveness and assertiveness when necessary.

I had the privilege of leading the department in a manner that exceeded everyone's expectations, resulting in remarkable success. This was evident from the anonymous 360-degree feedback survey I conducted, which revealed maximum satisfaction and a service grade of over 90 per cent. The entire department celebrated the achievements together, ensuring that credit was equally distributed among the entire team. Any requests, questions, doubts, or problems were treated as a top priority.

While work remained my primary focus and received my utmost attention, I also indulged in weekend celebrations. One of my passions is music, and I frequently attended shows by renowned artists such as Lionel Richie, Miles Davis, Madonna, Michael Jackson, Janet Jackson, Snoop Dogg, Stevie Wonder, Ray Charles, and many others. Sweden, fortunately, boasts a vibrant music scene, attracting world-class performers to its venues.

During one memorable evening, I had the opportunity to attend a captivating performance by a Stockholm Jazz band. Among the talented musicians, one individual, a Black bass guitarist, stood out like never before. His skill and artistry left a lasting impression on me, prompting me to seek him out after the show and express my admiration for his remarkable performance. I was pleasantly surprised to discover that his name was John, and he hailed from Gambia. We exchanged contact information, and two weeks later, he reached out, initiating a delightful conversation that allowed us to get to know each other better. As our conversations unfolded, John revealed that he was a part-time musician and a student at Stockholm University. He shared the story of his musical journey, which originated during his school days back in Gambia. Building upon our growing connection, John paid me a visit on a Sunday. Over a shared meal and a lengthy conversation, he introduced an intriguing proposition: starting a band. At first, I assumed he was joking, as I had never been part of a band nor possessed any musical abilities. The thought of becoming a lead singer seemed far-fetched, even in my wildest dreams.

However, John approached the idea with utmost seriousness, further solidifying the concept. A whirlwind of thoughts raced through my mind as I pondered what contribution I could make to a band. Nevertheless, John confidently proposed that I take on the role of the singer while he assembled a talented ensemble to handle various instruments. It turned out that John was a versatile musician himself, proficient in playing the rhythm and bass guitars, piano, keyboard, drums, and even the trumpet. His dedication to the band's idea was unwavering. Given my limited availability, I expressed my desire for the music group to be centred around enjoyment, shared interests, and a sense of amateurism. We agreed that it would be a project driven by passion rather than stringent professional commitments, allowing us to strike a balance with our respective schedules that might not allow for extensive practice time.

Following our decision to form a band, we embarked on planning the necessary equipment acquisitions. We identified instruments such as a digital keyboard, a drum machine, and rhythm and bass guitars as essential. It was important to us that the main objective of the music group would be to enjoy playing together at an amateur level. With these intentions set, we began to make progress. I took the initiative and invested in purchasing nearly all the instruments required for our endeavour. Additionally, I applied for a well-soundproofed rehearsal room located in the heart of Stockholm. This room featured a complete drum kit and offered 24/7 access, with the rent being covered by me. As the group's lead singer, I played a significant role in financing our endeavours. To prepare for my vocal responsibilities, I underwent training and dedicated myself to songwriting, which surprisingly yielded positive results. Taking on both lead vocals and songwriting, I ended up crafting a total of seventy-three songs.

We officially formed the band, choosing the name "Joy". John recruited other skilled musicians to join our ranks, and I found myself standing before the microphone with pages of lyrics in hand. We diligently rehearsed every other weekend, exploring genres such as R&B, soul, hip-hop, and occasional reggae influences. The band was a source of joy and we thoroughly enjoyed the experience. I never imagined that I would sing, let alone assume the role of lead vocalist in a group. Nevertheless, we persisted, and our hard work paid off as we completed thirteen songs that were recorded as our debut album. Gradually, we took our music to the stage, performing gigs in various restaurants. It was a surreal experience for me, as I reflected on how far we had come. At times, I questioned whether I desired to pursue this path further, but John's unwavering commitment propelled the music project to new heights.

The music industry in Stockholm was notorious for rampant gossip and the allure of securing a coveted recording deal with a record company. However, the reality was that these companies often took advantage of artists' talents, reaping substantial profits while leaving them with a meagre share of the revenue. Stockholm's music scene was a tight-knit and well-connected clique, where many artists were willing to sacrifice everything for a chance to sign a record deal. I had personally witnessed artists being used and mistreated for years before finally securing their first record deal. This topic became a regular point of discussion whenever we met.

Despite our passion for music, I made it clear to the group that I would not abandon my job for a music career. I remained committed to being available for weekend gigs in and around the Stockholm area. We collectively decided against sending our recorded demos to any record company. It was widely known that these companies would reject demos but steal a copy of your music to later hear it on radio stations with new vocals. The music industry operated without regulation and possessed significant power, making legal action a futile endeavour. Therefore, we held onto our music, avoiding the potential exploitation that could come with signing a record deal. I had a close American friend named Derrick, a well-known jazz/soul artist who sadly passed away. As artists, we supported each other. I would attend all his shows free of charge, appreciating the mutual respect within the music community. One Saturday, Derrick was scheduled to perform in Gamla Stan, the Old Town located in the heart of Stockholm, not far from the parliament building.

And three close friends from Sweden decided to attend Derrick's performance. We all gathered at the home of one of the girls who lived in town, parked our cars at her place, and then took the underground to the venue. The show turned out to be a tremendous success, and we enjoyed a delightful dinner followed by an amazing night out. As the clock struck two in the morning, we made the collective decision to leave. Exiting the club, we walked a short distance of five minutes to reach the underground station. However, our peaceful departure was abruptly interrupted when a group of six individuals with shaved heads appeared, hurling verbal abuse in my direction and threatening to end my life. Despite the chaotic scene with insults and shouting exchanged between both parties, I maintained my composure, acutely aware of the escalating tension and its potential consequences.

Instinctively, I positioned myself against a nearby wall, ensuring no one could approach me from behind. The tallest individual within the group menacingly brandished a gleaming silver pistol, firing a single shot into the air while emphatically warning that any further remarks from me would result in a fatal outcome. The firing of the gun only intensified the commotion as the girls accompanying me reacted with heightened agitation, responding vociferously to the aggressors. Among the skinheads, one individual exhibited signs of extreme anxiety, displaying nervous behaviour, sweating profusely, and relentlessly urging the person who had discharged the firearm, saying, "Let's do it, man! Let's just kill him!" persistently advocating for my demise.

The girls vehemently asserted that they would inevitably face arrest and spend a significant portion of their lives behind bars if they were to carry out the violent act, emphasizing that while their lives would be forever altered, the world would persist. Amid this chaotic and perilous situation, the minutes ticking away relentlessly, a sudden influx of people began to arrive as the train's arrival time drew nearer. Witnessing the growing crowd, the entire group of skinheads abruptly shifted their demeanour, adopting an innocent facade and blending in with the crowd as if nothing had occurred. However, one of the girls refused to back down, persistently berating and shaming them in front of the onlookers as the train finally pulled up. Addressing me directly, the tallest individual brazenly remarked, "Where do you live? We'll come to visit you." Seizing the moment, I responded with a calculated statement, "Just follow me, and you'll discover my address."

Although they did not board the same train as us, they likely awaited the next one as we departed from the Old Town. Incidents like this are distressingly commonplace, with unprovoked assaults and even fatalities rampant in many parts of Europe. Neo-Nazis frequently operate in organized groups, engaging in dangerous behaviour and tragically claiming innocent lives. Law-abiding citizens endure daily harassment and threats, be it at their workplaces, public spaces, schools, or even within their neighbourhoods. Racism permeates society, devoid of a place in any civilized realm, especially in the twenty-first century. Regrettably, politicians, particularly those leaning towards the right end of the political spectrum, demonstrate little interest in enacting protective legislation for marginalized communities.

The gravity of violence perpetrated by right-wing groups against minorities demands serious attention from society. Each year, numerous individuals of foreign backgrounds, particularly Africans, fall victim to unprovoked attacks in Europe, incidents that often fail to make headlines. This reality highlights the importance for minorities to remain vigilant about their whereabouts and actions in public spaces. A violent racist assault can befall any black man at any time, in any location. Discrimination is an ever-present burden endured by anyone with foreign features, whether it be black hair or black or brown skin. I once had a black friend who was born in Stockholm and aspired to venture into entrepreneurship. Despite completing his university education, he encountered insurmountable obstacles in securing a job. Instead, he obtained a loan from a bank and took the bold step of starting a dry-cleaning business. He moved into a new building where I also worked.

For months, he diligently operated the business, but not a single customer walked through his door. He shared his experiences of individuals entering his shop with clothes in hand, only to abruptly leave the moment they laid eyes on him. The huge signboard outside did not disclose that a black man owned and ran the establishment. Therefore, customers would come into the shop but just avert their gaze and leave upon seeing him behind the counter. Plunging further into debt with no viable alternatives, he was forced to sell the business at a significantly reduced price to someone else who subsequently achieved success in running it. Instances occur where individuals visit a bank or a company, encounter a black employee and subsequently call and complain that they won't want to interact with a black person during future visits. A sad situation, but real! These accounts underscore the pervasive nature of discrimination and the barriers faced by minorities in various professional and social settings. Such experiences highlight the urgent need for systemic change and a concerted effort to foster inclusivity and equality in all facets of society.

The grievances expressed in these accounts have been extensively documented by investigative journalists over time. As a black man residing in Europe, I have learned to cultivate resilience, tolerance, and self-defence while also navigating the arduous task of disregarding instances of injustice, intimidation, and prejudice. To exist in a society tainted by racism, one must adapt and find ways to cope, even though it remains an issue that will persist indefinitely. It is disheartening to acknowledge that discrimination and injustice exist in other societies, such as those found in Africa, based on tribe and caste. However, in the Western world, where they pride themselves on being the epitome of civilization, modernity, and democracy, one would expect racism and injustice to be minimal or non-existent. We had hoped that after centuries of institutionalized racism, it would have been eradicated by now.

Disliking or harbouring strong hatred towards someone solely based on their inherent characteristics reveals a deeply flawed perspective in the eyes of the beholder. A sensible and fair-minded individual should evaluate others based on the quality of their character and behaviour rather than the colour of their skin. The most deplorable form of human behaviour occurs when individuals are denied livelihoods, positions, or opportunities purely due to their race or gender. I consider myself fortunate to have attained a prominent position, although it came with numerous challenges. I owe my ability to retain this job to the support and assistance provided by my CEO. However, I was only able to succeed in this role due to the professionalism and maturity I consistently demonstrated.

When I assumed the leadership role as the supervisor of Europe's fifth largest and most advanced warehouse facility at that time, I was appalled by the excessive waste production, which reached approximately forty-five tonnes per month. Recognizing the gravity of the situation, I embarked on reducing waste by fifty per cent within twelve months. Taking decisive action, I organized a meeting where we collectively brainstormed ideas and garnered a wealth of suggestions for waste reduction. Collaborating with a select group, including our dedicated secretary, we meticulously sifted through the ideas, carefully evaluating their feasibility until we settled on the most viable solution. The implementation of this successful project not only yielded cost savings but also demonstrated our commitment to environmental preservation. The entire team rejoiced in this achievement as it was a collective effort involving almost everyone in some capacity.

Given my prominence in the role, I constantly found myself surrounded by numerous individuals seeking my attention. To manage this influx of people, I sometimes avoided frequenting the main shopping mall due to the sheer volume of individuals wanting to engage with me along the way. A simple shopping trip that should have taken thirty minutes would invariably extend to three hours or more. Whether it was store managers, high-ranking council members, diligent security guards, or owners of restaurants and shops, all were familiar with my identity. To foster closer relationships with these individuals, I employed various techniques such as remembering names and initiating conversations on topics of interest. Additionally, I recognized the importance of attentive listening and providing maximum focus to ensure that everyone felt valued and heard.

Living just a short distance from Karin's place, barely three minutes away, I occasionally took a little time out of my schedule to visit her and enjoy a cup of coffee together. Karin had a passion for baking, which she thoroughly enjoyed. One chilly winter day, I noticed that despite the snowy and icy conditions, she was wearing lightweight summer shoes with no grip on the soles. Concerned for her safety, I urged her to switch to proper winter footwear. It seemed that she either ignored my advice or simply forgot about it, as she continued to wear those unsuitable shoes. Karin was always known for her impeccable dress, disciplined demeanour, and eloquent speech. However, approximately two weeks later, around nine in the evening, she left to go to the petrol station. Upon her return, she drove her car towards the underground entrance, attempting to reach the keyhole pole.

She struggled to extend her hand far enough to open it. In a decision fuelled by determination, she stepped out of the car onto the icy ground, but tragically, she lost her footing and fell with great force, her head colliding with the unforgiving concrete. She immediately lost consciousness, lying near the car door on the icy surface, enveloped in darkness. Meanwhile, her car door remained open, and the engine continued to run. Fortunately, an observant individual happened upon the scene. Spotting Karin's car parked in the middle of the road, engine still running, with the door wide open but no one inside, he cautiously manoeuvred his vehicle to the left side of Karin's car. It was then that the person noticed her lying on the icy ground. Without hesitation, the concerned neighbour rushed to her side, lending a helping hand and promptly manoeuvring her car into the safety of the garage.

Subsequently, the kind-hearted individual contacted Karin's youngest daughter, who happened to be a doctor residing in the southern part of Stockholm. The daughter swiftly made her way to Karin's residence. Upon arrival, she carefully examined her Mum's condition and decided to transport her directly to Karolinska Teaching Hospital, a mere twenty-minute drive away. The following morning, just as I was accustomed to waking up around six o'clock, an unfamiliar number flashed on my phone screen, stirring a sense of unease within me. It was an agitating moment, but when I answered, the voice on the other end was filled with distress. Without uttering a word initially, the caller finally managed to say, "Mum, Salomon, Mum!" Alarmed, I anxiously inquired, "What happened?" The tearful voice proceeded to explain that Karin had slipped on the ice at the garage entrance, striking her head on the unforgiving concrete. They were at the hospital attending to her.

Promptly, I took a swift shower, contacted my secretary to manage any urgent matters, and swiftly drove to the hospital. I spent over an hour there, but Karin was asleep, unaware of my presence. The situation weighed heavily upon us all, and her daughter informed me that although disoriented, Karin's condition was stable. After concluding my work for the day, I returned to the hospital to see her. She greeted me with a somewhat perplexed smile, inquiring about the person who had brought her to the hospital. It became apparent that she was still struggling with disorientation. Witnessing her in that state broke my heart. After a couple of days, she was transferred from the hospital to a nearby care home, close to her residence. In the ensuing weeks, I visited Karin at the care home every other day, witnessing a rapid decline in her mental state within a short period. The situation was very distressing, leaving me deeply concerned for her well-being.

However, amidst the decline in her mental state, Karin still possessed the ability to recognize me, setting me apart from the rest of the family. Yet, as time went on, she faced increasing difficulties in identifying her children, which proved to be a challenging situation for them to handle. It would often take her a while to recall their names, sometimes even needing to ask who they were. One of her children expressed anger and frustration, unable to comprehend how a Mum could forget the names of her offspring. Karin would inquire with the staff at the care home about whether I would be visiting again on the following day, as her memory continued to fade. She was no longer the same person I had known throughout the years leading up to the drastic changes in her life.

After spending eight months in the care home, I received a phone call one day, delivering the heartbreaking news of Karin's early morning passing. It was a deeply painful and tragic loss for me. The family approached me and asked which belongings of Karin's I would like to keep. I chose to take her new Nissan Cherry, a stunning brown-coloured vehicle and utilized it as my winter car for several years to come. The remaining possessions were sold, with the proceeds divided amongst the family members. Eventually, the house was also sold, and the proceeds were distributed accordingly. As I devoted more time to my work, my involvement in musical activities began to taper off. However, the NGO continued to thrive, particularly with the inclusion of a UN organization from the neighbouring county. This partnership increased membership, enabling the organization to provide additional space for more children and teachers, expanding the reach and impact of the project.

The passing of Karin was an immensely challenging experience for me, given the closeness we shared. One of the most difficult aspects of death is the profound silence that follows. Someone whom one conversed with daily, and shared countless moments with over the years is suddenly gone forever, and it is an incredibly hard reality to face. I experienced similar emotions when I lost my Mum and later my Dad. The realization that we will never see each other again, that their voices, faces, and physical presence are forever absent apart from pictures, weighs heavily. This is especially poignant when it concerns a Mum, who gave birth to me, nurtured, nourished me and ensured that I grew up to become the best version of myself. Although it has been a considerable amount of time since my parents passed away, the thought of them is always refreshing, as I firmly believe that their spirits remain with me eternally.

In addition to my commitments at work, I actively participated in weekend workshops, conferences, and seminars organized by the United Nations. These events provided valuable opportunities to collaborate with the Afghanistan Committee in Stockholm, focusing on the important cause of female education. The civil society in Sweden is vibrant, enlightened, and highly engaged. People believe that their small contributions can make a meaningful impact and bring positive change to the lives of even the most disadvantaged children, fostering a better and more peaceful world. The country is brimming with civil society organizations, each striving to achieve excellence in various fields such as healthcare, education, women's empowerment, and youth employment in developing countries. These collective efforts instil a sense of belonging and create a powerful movement of solidarity that aims to reshape global inequalities.

Having assumed the leadership role in the department, a position I never envisioned myself in, it was my boldness, confidence, and desire for personal growth that propelled me forward. The CEO recognized my potential and capabilities through my ideas, writing, and speaking, placing their trust in me. Consequently, I also believed that I was more than qualified for the position. While diversity is often touted as a positive and essential aspect of any workplace, the practical implementation of this concept remains elusive for many HR departments. In reality, diversity tends to be relegated to the bottom of the priority list rather than being placed at the forefront or integrated into the company's core values. Merely advocating for diversity without taking substantial action is rendered meaningless.

Unfortunately, many companies engage in what I refer to as 'Window-dressing diversity', where a representative from a minority group is put forward as the face of diversity, giving the appearance of inclusion without substantial change. For corporate diversity to truly flourish, it must permeate every level and sector of the company. A workplace that embraces diversity reaps the benefits of enhanced creativity, innovation, understanding, and productivity. Additionally, diversity plays a significant role in fulfilling corporate social responsibility. When a company's workforce reflects the diverse makeup of the society it operates in, it becomes more closely associated and connected with the community. Over time, as I settled into my role as the department leader, a sense of stability, heightened productivity, and a harmonious atmosphere prevailed. We made consistent progress in addressing inherent issues and overcoming backlogs, ensuring a positive trajectory for the department.

As time went on, the initial protests and animosity I faced from colleagues dissipated. Internal recruitment within a company can often trigger anger and resentment, which can have significant implications such as diminished credibility, a demotivated workforce, and weakened authority or adherence to established rules. To regain control in such situations, it is crucial to foster understanding and engage all stakeholders as equal partners, while ensuring that the company's final decisions hold weight. I consider myself fortunate to have gained the wholehearted support of the CEO. Ultimately, the Union also rallied behind me once they uncovered the true motives behind the protests, which stemmed from a combination of jealousy and occasional racially charged comments. Amid such conflicts, a new leader needs to maintain professionalism, composure, and a forward-looking approach.

Decisiveness and assertiveness are equally important qualities to navigate through such challenges and address the concerns of all stakeholders while safeguarding the overall interests of the company. One particular type of conflict I encountered in my role was with engineers—experts who often believe their knowledge places them above departmental heads or rules, leading to conflicts between management and specialists. In my view, experts should always be at the forefront, utilizing their expertise to ensure flawless operations. However, an expert who also assumes a leadership position in both capacities may struggle to fully leverage their expertise. As the head of a department, my responsibilities encompass administrative duties, personnel and workforce management, internal and external communication, and directing efforts towards achieving the company's goals and objectives.

Assuming a top position entails immense responsibilities. Fostering teamwork, building relationships, and promoting harmony, respect, understanding, and dedication among colleagues are crucial elements in achieving a smoothly functioning system, creating a pleasant work environment, and realizing corporate goals. As a leader, I approached the task of managing engineers with a foundation of mutual respect. I refrained from intervening in their work unless it directly related to external contacts. They possessed the knowledge and skills necessary to perform their tasks, and I empowered them by granting them the freedom and autonomy to excel in their respective roles. In doing so, the boundaries of authority were clearly defined, and I ensured that nobody intentionally overstepped their limits. Establishing a relationship based on mutual respect enabled everyone to understand and operate within their designated boundaries. I took great satisfaction in my work, my position, and the collective achievements we accomplished as a team.

During one of our successful Friday coffee sessions, I introduced a large wooden box called 'the yellow box'. This box served as a repository for products that were unsuitable for regular delivery but still fit for consumption. Previously, these products would have been discarded into a rubbish container. However, items such as coffee, biscuits, various types of chocolate, cheese, and other confectioneries with misprinted dates or those that had fallen on the floor fit for consumption were now placed in the yellow box. Each worker was allowed to enjoy unlimited access to the contents of the yellow box and could also take a limited amount home. The yellow box gained immense popularity, to the extent that even high-ranking officials from the main office would visit the yellow box to partake in its offerings.

There were instances when I noticed senior executives discreetly making their way to the yellow box, thinking they went unnoticed. However, these individuals had always been kind to me, and I preferred to maintain a positive relationship with them. Initially, the yellow box was intended solely for our department, but its growing popularity led to the interest of others outside our team. Nonetheless, the company had a personnel boutique where employees could purchase various products at discounted prices. The Christmas season, being the busiest time of the year, called for increased efforts in delivering as many products as possible. Therefore, I had to ensure effective contingency planning, a readily available workforce, and a smoothly functioning supply chain system.

Timely delivery played a crucial role in maintaining efficiency. The Christmas buffet dinner, accompanied by music and delightful presents, was an event eagerly anticipated by all. It was the most joyous time of the year, and the company had a tradition of generously gifting valuable presents to its employees. Additionally, I found myself participating in the Stockholm Marathon each year. Completing a full marathon is a significant personal challenge that requires determination and unwavering dedication. Training for many kilometres in preparation for the race is essential. The Stockholm marathon is one of the city's most popular public events.

Regardless of the suffering, agony, and distress experienced during a race, crossing the finish line and receiving a medal is an incredible moment for every runner. I once had a memorable experience in Washington DC, where I enjoyed a three-week holiday and spent hours cycling with friends every weekend. Upon returning to Stockholm just before the Marathon weekend, I spontaneously decided to participate in the race, despite not having had the opportunity to train specifically for it. Surprisingly, it turned out to be my personal best time, completing the Marathon in two hours and fifty minutes. I strongly believe that cycling is an excellent way to stay in shape.

On another occasion, while out for a run near my home, I witnessed a group of teenagers hastily fleeing as they caught sight of me. Curious, I approached the spot where they had been and discovered a small fire near the library window. Reacting swiftly, I grabbed some branches from a nearby tree and extinguished the flames. Without encountering the teenagers again, I continued my run and returned home. However, after a few hours, there was a knock on my door. Peering through the doorhole, I noticed two police officers. I welcomed them inside when they identified themselves and asked for permission to enter. They informed me that a neighbour had reported seeing me starting the fire at the library, and they had visited the scene where they detected the smell of fresh fire. Calmly, I received them and provided a detailed explanation of what had transpired and the timeline of events.

After giving my statement to the police officers, I noticed their composure and trust in me. They inquired about my occupation, and upon witnessing the well-organized manner in which I lived, they had no doubts about the credibility of my statement. They could discern that someone of my calibre would not engage in such a crime. As our conversation progressed, we ended up having a pleasant chat about the marathon race, and it seemed like they were making excuses to prolong their visit. Nevertheless, I understood that they were simply carrying out their noble duty.

During the harsh and freezing winters of Sweden, particularly in the early 1990s when temperatures could drop below minus 20 degrees Celsius, I began to notice that the hair on my head was thinning at an alarming rate. This rapid hair loss started around my thirtieth birthday, and before long, I realized that very little hair was left in the middle of my head. It became evident to me that I was becoming bald. During a holiday in the USA in the early 1990s, I found myself spending many hours engrossed in daytime TV talk shows such as

Jerry Springer, Ricky Lake, Montel Williams, Oprah Winfrey, Sally Jesse Raphael, and others. The allure of reality TV, with its human stories and captivating narratives, captivated my attention. However, what surprised me the most was seeing Montel Williams with his clean-shaven head. At the time, black men predominantly sported Afro hairstyles, so witnessing a black TV host with a bald head was quite unexpected. It was later reported in the news that Montel Williams was recognized as one of America's sexiest men.

The survey conducted by a Hollywood magazine revealed that women found Montel Williams attractive and sexy with his baldness. This story not only boosted my confidence but also instilled a sense of acceptance and trendiness among many black men who were experiencing hair loss or were already bald. Inspired by this, I decided to embrace the clean-shaven look and started shaving my head. To my delight, my friends appreciated my new appearance and even remarked that it suited me better than having hair. I soon noticed that many black men, including those in the NBA and R&B musicians, were also adopting the clean-shaven style. Over the past twenty years or so, shaving my head has become my preferred choice, and I couldn't be happier with it.

Living on my own and keeping myself busy with work, my involvement in the NGO, running, and playing music with the band, I often find solace in solitude. When I return home after a long and hectic day, I sometimes neglect the telephone and simply desire to relax in a peaceful and tranquil environment. I had a large warm rug in the middle of my sitting room, adorned with small pillows on the side. Taking the time to lie down on the rug for over an hour restores my balance and energy, providing me with comfort and a pleasant evening. I enjoy preparing a nice dinner, tending to household chores, and ensuring that everything is in order. Following my divorce from Sana, I reverted to my familiar solitary ways, which have always been my comfort zone since childhood. I have a distaste for noise and appreciate the serenity that solitude brings.

Living on my own and cherishing my moments of solitude, I prioritized and guarded my quietness. After years of living with someone, I had come to appreciate and value these peaceful moments. When Sana left, I took the opportunity to clean up the storage area of my apartment on a beautiful Sunday. While entering the building from the rubbish area, where we sort out the trash, I encountered an elderly couple, likely in their eighties, just as I swiped my keycard to open the door. The man inquired about whether I lived there, and I replied, "Upstairs, I live here." Surprised, he asked if I had just moved in. I clarified, "No, I've been living here for almost three years." He said that they had never heard any noise coming from my apartment and had assumed it was vacant.

Due to my busy schedule during the weekdays with work and my commitments to the UN and orphanage NGO on weekends, I had limited spare time to interact with the neighbours or be seen around their houses. The short periods I spent at home were mainly dedicated to work, reading, or being on the phone. Despite being a member of a band where we played loud music, I didn't particularly enjoy the noise. There was hardly any music played at home, even though I owned an extensive Yamaha huge stereo set. Our musical journey as a band didn't progress beyond recording an album of thirteen original songs, performing a few gigs, and offering me a chance to showcase my skills as a songwriter and lead singer.

I have always believed that nothing is impossible to learn and master, a belief I held since childhood. The key factors in achieving mastery are dedication, interest, patience, and a clear focus. I applied these principles when setting any objectives, understanding that proficiency is crucial for personal and professional growth. I firmly believe that when you know what you want and have a clear sense of direction and dedication, achieving those objectives becomes a possibility. Giving up on your goals leads to failure, so I learned from my past mistakes, approached new challenges with passion, and embraced the valuable lessons along the way. Passion is what fuels my drive and keeps me motivated to succeed. Achieving success in one endeavour serves as a great source of motivation for me to seek new opportunities and challenges. The ability to learn quickly and adapt to change is essential for leaders in today's fast-paced workplace.

Lifelong learning has become a necessity as technology, globalization, just-in-time supply chains, and other rapid systems dominate our professional environments. I recall an incident when I asked a team member if he would be willing to work on a Saturday. Unfortunately, this person was not inclined to go beyond his regular duties. He had a fixed routine, arriving at exactly nine and leaving at five, without a minute more or less. For over thirty years, he occupied the same seat near the window, which was always reserved for him in our department.

He hailed from Finland, and I informed him about the need to work on Saturdays to clear pending deliveries. In response, he adamantly refused, stating, "No! I don't want to work on Saturday." Despite reminding him about the additional compensation he would receive, his refusal remained resolute. However, an intriguing turn of events unfolded when he arrived at the office on Monday, carrying his bank book after breakfast. He approached my office and said, "Let me show you something," revealing his bank book. To my disbelief, I saw an astounding sum of over one million Swedish Krona in his account. I had to verify the figures repeatedly, as I couldn't fathom the reality before me. Doubting if the bank book was counterfeit, I inquired, only to confirm its authenticity. He then declared, "You see, I don't need to work on Saturdays because of money," before leaving.

He was a man of few words and rarely went beyond the call of duty, simply working and returning home regardless of the circumstances. I made many attempts to involve him in various tasks at work, delegating responsibilities, and encouraging him to share ideas, and actively participate. However, he remained an extreme introvert, unwilling to lend a hand or collaborate actively in any teamwork. The revelation that he was a millionaire, unknown to us, came as an enormous surprise. Despite lacking any other notable skills apart from his thirty-year-long work experience, to me, he possessed an extraordinary talent for saving money. While we couldn't harness his secret ability to its full potential, he displayed an unwavering reluctance to engage in anything beyond his primary duties.

However, it is always advisable to foster a team environment everyone's contributions are equally valued. By including and engaging the entire team, we can unveil hidden talents that will benefit the job as a whole. It may require effort and patience to involve individuals who are naturally introverted or less inclined to participate actively. However, the success of uniting people towards a common purpose yields greater benefits and reduces blame when things go awry. From the beginning, I made it a priority to curtail office politics. As a regular employee within the department, I had already witnessed the detrimental effects of gossip, quarrels, and petty behaviour that tainted the atmosphere.

Eliminating such toxic behaviour took time and effort. I treated all staff members equally, refrained from listening to one-sided accounts during conflicts, and consciously disregarded any gossip or hearsay. I believed in the principle of "if you don't have anything nice to say, don't say anything at all" when it came to speaking about others. Gossiping and backbiting were discouraged, and I strived to create a harmonious workplace where ethics guided my actions. Work became my steadfast companion.

One day, while parking my car near the department, I noticed someone standing there, seemingly waiting for someone. As they approached me, they began speaking in Swedish.

He introduced himself as a Gambian who had heard about me within the company and expressed a desire to meet and get acquainted. I was pleased to meet him. He had arrived in Sweden approximately four years ago and had recently started working in the company after marrying a Swedish woman. I encountered him again in the canteen during lunch on a Friday, but we were unable to have a conversation. However, a month later, my secretary informed me that someone from the company had been tragically killed over the weekend at a restaurant near the train station. Later that day, I received a call explaining that the victim was the same Gambian individual I had met at the parking area a month prior. I was utterly shocked to hear the news. They later revealed that he had been intoxicated and engaged in a fight with someone, who ultimately stabbed him in the heart before leaving his body near the waterway close to the train station.

He was a vibrant and passionate person, probably around thirty years old. This incident reinforced my belief in the importance of knowing where to go, how to behave, and when to disengage. Walking away can be a powerful tool in defusing conflicts, particularly with unfamiliar individuals. I have come to realize that winning an argument holds little significance when there is a clash of ideas. Over the years, I have learned the value of letting go. Even when I know that I am right, it is better to preserve the other person's dignity and separate amicably, avoiding humiliation and anger. Trying to prove oneself right against others only fosters avoidance, sometimes resentment and animosity. When confronted with a racist attack, although demeaning, walking away remains the best option.

Tragically, numerous young black men lose their lives on the streets of Europe while futilely resisting injustice. Violent racism pervades Western societies, sometimes manifesting in unexpected places such as the police force, courts, and educational institutions. One summer, I travelled to Hamburg to purchase a car as car prices are cheaper in Germany than in Sweden. Upon my arrival, I checked into a hotel and decided to have dinner at a nearby restaurant. Subsequently, I took a leisurely walk along a pedestrian street before retiring for the night. The street was illuminated, bustling with people, and the weather was dry and cool. Suddenly, chaos erupted as I witnessed people running and screaming in my direction. They were fleeing from neo-Nazis who were viciously attacking individuals with chains and knives. Reacting swiftly, I turned back and joined the panicked crowd in a desperate attempt to escape. In my frantic search for safety, I spotted a police station on my left and hurriedly sought refuge inside.

A police officer stood behind the counter, and I quickly informed him about the ongoing violence perpetrated by neo-Nazis. To my astonishment, he simply glanced at me and pointed towards the door, callously stating, "If you don't want that, don't come here!" This encounter served as a reminder that people still judge individuals based on the colour of their skin rather than the content of their character. Despite these distressing experiences, I remained committed to my work with NGOs, particularly in orphanages, and actively participated in collaborative events such as meetings, conferences, and seminars, mostly held on weekends. Establishing structured plans for my evenings allowed me to effectively organize my activities.

Over time, I grew increasingly comfortable and confident in my work, striving to reduce waste and enhance efficiency through the implementation of lean practices. As the days passed, everything improved. During this period, I had the fortune of meeting my beloved wife, this time a Gambian who proved to be the perfect match for me, igniting the desire to build a life and family together. It had been nearly twenty years since I had experienced such a profound connection with someone. The prospect of spending the rest of my life with a compatible partner added immeasurable value and purpose to my existence. Initiating a relationship is relatively easy, but nurturing and sustaining a successful relationship demands unwavering attention, love, care, sacrifice, understanding, consideration, empathy, and mutual respect.

Amidst my numerous commitments, I began to ponder which activities I should prioritize and potentially let go of to devote more time and energy to my new relationship. Both of us were elated by the love we shared, and eventually, we decided to marry. My partner entered my life at a time when I was fully engrossed in hard work, striving for personal and professional goals, and nurturing hopes for a promising future. We engaged in deep conversations for weeks, aligning our aspirations, and ambitions, and envisioning our shared future. I had a well-appointed study where I carried out most of my report-writing work from home, and reading management and self-development books remained an integral part of my daily routine. My partner actively participated in most of the endeavours I was involved in. This was important to ensure that she understood my work-oriented nature and to explore how our relationship could evolve accordingly, with mutual understanding and support for each other.

To prioritize my growing family, I decided to reduce my involvement in UN engagements at the Stockholm UN branch, reserving weekends for quality time with my partner at home. However, I continued to actively participate in local NGO meetings, although they were not as frequent. We relocated to a larger apartment in the same area, which provided more space for our expanding family. My partner also secured a job close to our home, facilitating convenience and work-life balance. As time passed, we were blessed with the arrival of our baby girl. The day of her birth marked the first time in over thirteen years that I was absent from work. In the afternoon, we drove to the main hospital in Uppsala, where my wife gave birth in the evening. I stood by her side, assisting throughout the delivery process. Witnessing the intense pain she endured during labour, my heart overflowed with sympathy, and tears welled up in my eyes. When the baby finally arrived, I couldn't contain my emotions and cried tears of joy.

Perplexed by my tears, the doctor inquired about the reason behind my emotional response. I replied, "It's evident that I am overjoyed, but I am also thinking about the world she will grow up in." I expressed my concerns about the challenges and discrimination faced by individuals with dark skin in this part of the world. The doctor, acknowledging the truth in my words, agreed, saying, "Yes, you are right." Despite centuries of progress, gender equality still eludes us in various sectors. We decided to honour my beloved Mum by naming our daughter after her and celebrated the occasion with a christening ceremony. Becoming a Dad has been the most profound and fulfilling experience of my life. I felt a deep sense of completeness and contentment throughout the journey. Taking care of our baby also brings back memories of my childhood, when I assisted my Mum in caring for my younger siblings. Watching our child grow every week, month, and year is an incredibly thrilling and rewarding experience for every parent.

The responsibilities of parenting encompass a wide range of tasks, from sacrificing personal needs to providing care, nourishment, and clothing, and teaching valuable lessons as our children progress through different stages of development. It is an intricate and sometimes challenging journey that can evoke a variety of emotions. I became extremely protective and attentive to my little girl, quickly responding to her cries and ensuring her well-being. Every action she took was closely observed to prevent any harm. I would cradle her until she fell asleep and constantly strive to create a comfortable environment for her. To be honest, I found myself embodying more of a Mumly role than a typical Dad. When she was just weeks old, I purchased a special computer programme designed for infants, featuring captivating colours and accompanying music, which would grab her attention as she followed the colour patterns. She adored it, and it became a source of fascination for her.

Additionally, I prioritized her health by encouraging her to grab a water bottle, a carrot, or a cucumber instead of offering candies or soft drinks. I believed in instilling healthy habits from an early age. Soon enough, it was time for her to start kindergarten. It was challenging to leave her there in the mornings as she would cry, expressing her reluctance. However, as time passed, she began to enjoy her time at kindergarten. One day, her teacher told me, "Your daughter is like my deputy. She consistently helps and shows kindness to the other children all the time." Those words filled us with joy and pride. In Sweden, I have friends who believe that starting a family or having a child would jeopardize their careers, and they prefer to keep a pet, typically a dog, instead. However, for me, having a child has been the most fulfilling experience, one that I would even sacrifice my career for. I hold the firm belief that humans are incomparable to animals, and the love and connection we share with our children are unparalleled.

Indeed, individuals have the freedom to choose their paths in life, and it is essential to respect their choices. I am aware that many people in Africa, specifically in the Gambia, may strongly disagree with certain lifestyle choices.

It is important to recognize that women have the right to autonomy over their bodies, and it is their freedom to decide whether or not to have children. Respecting women's rights is a fundamental principle in establishing a just, productive, and modern society.

These fundamental rights should be prioritized above any other social systems or beliefs. Human rights are about promoting freedom and empowering society to reach its full potential without fear or constraint.

It is disheartening that many years have passed since the signing of the Universal Declaration of Human Rights and the ratification of the Convention on the Elimination of All Forms of Discrimination Against Women (1979), yet gender equality is still far from being fully achieved.

It is crucial for countries, including The Gambia and other African nations, to uphold their commitments and hold themselves accountable for the ratified conventions regarding women's rights. Despite these commitments, setbacks in women's rights persist. To address this issue, it is important to incorporate the teachings of these rights into early education and continue raising awareness through various media outlets. By ensuring that people are knowledgeable about their rights, we can bridge the gap between theory and practice, leading to effective implementation. Traditional beliefs and practices that infringe upon the rights of girls and women in The Gambia are deeply concerning. As the country grows and develops, it is crucial to enlighten society and empower the vulnerable. No individual should be left behind in the pursuit of gender equality and human rights.

As my family responsibilities grew, I found myself increasingly engrossed in caring for my loved ones, leading me to step back from my involvement in music. Family life demanded a significant portion of my time, and the responsibilities of the NGO work were also demanding. Consequently, I decided to prioritize my family and relinquished my role as the Chairman of the NGO after many years of dedicated service. There were concerns that the organization and its work would suffer without my involvement. With an extensive network of influential individuals, particularly in Ghana and Sweden, including within the SIDA office and local networks, I was seen as a valuable asset. Additionally, my fluency in spoken and written English further enhanced my contributions. However, finding a suitable successor proved challenging as no one seemed willing to take on the role. Despite my efforts to convince a few individuals, I was unable to secure a successor for the position.

I informed the executive that I needed some time to consider stepping down from my position. After discussing it with my wife, we ultimately decided that I should resign as the chairman of the NGO. Since we could only secure the meeting hall on Saturdays, we gathered again to discuss the matter. I arrived with my resignation letter, citing family reasons for my decision. However, I also presented a proposition to join forces with our sister NGO in the neighbouring county of Sollentuna. We had a history of collaboration, exchanging ideas, and organizing conferences together. The chairwoman, whom I knew well and considered a good friend, was a high school Math teacher.

The proposal was presented, put to vote, and subsequently approved by the general body the following Saturday. I accepted a new role as a regular member and offered my assistance to the organization in any way possible. This included facilitating membership registrations, contributing to project work, and transferring all assets to another UN organization in a legal manner. I fulfilled my promise to support the NGO to the best of my abilities. Taking on the responsibility of organizing meetings, creating agendas, making evening phone calls, selling Sunday coffees at the church, and promoting UNICEF cards came to an end. It felt like a huge weight had been lifted off my shoulders. However, entrusting the organization to capable hands, especially someone I knew well, filled me with hope and reassurance that the orphanage would continue to thrive and provide a better future for the children we served.

Several months later, the organization received a remarkable contribution in the form of a donated bus, which was subsequently shipped to Africa through freight services. The organization's progress continued to flourish as it successfully secured annual project grants from SIDA, ensuring the seamless operation of the orphanage. With these responsibilities well-managed, I found myself able to prioritize my family, work, and personal well-being, including carving out time for exercise. During this period, my partner's sister, residing in the UK, engaged in numerous discussions with us about life and living in that country.

Gradually, my partner and I made a joint decision to embark on a bold and adventurous journey by moving to the UK. It was a blend of nervousness and excitement—a daring leap of faith. We were willing to leave behind my good and stable job in Sweden and embrace the potential of a less unknown and financially less rewarding one to forge a new life in the United Kingdom. Nevertheless, I was prepared to make the sacrifice. The primary source of my confidence in this life-altering choice stemmed from my unwavering trust and faith in my partner.

A couple of times, I have experienced moments of doubt whether leaving my beloved job and home in Sweden was the right decision. However, after thorough contemplation and careful planning, I began to believe that I was indeed making the right choice. When I considered the potential positive impact that achieving my plans could have, not just for me but for my entire family and the individuals whose lives I could influence, it reaffirmed my belief. Our decision was also influenced by profound reflections on encounters with racism in Sweden, which we desperately wished to shield our daughter from. The weight of those thoughts brought tears to my eyes when she was born, and ultimately became the primary motivation behind my acceptance to leave Sweden.

Writing and submitting my resignation letter was not an easy task. Without providing detailed explanations about my future endeavours, many, including my secretary, thought I had gone mad! However, my CEO, acknowledging the racism I had faced, understood that it may have played a role in my decision. I simply informed him that I was leaving the country with my family. The transition to the United Kingdom went smoothly, and now I am preparing to chronicle my experiences in my upcoming book, which will delve into life in the UK, my reflections, my political journey, and my unwavering commitment to continue to learn and grow.

The bitter experiences of racism that I have endured living in the Western world are something I would never wish upon anyone. Sadly, it seems that significant changes in attitudes may not occur in the coming decades, and I must come to terms with the fact that my daughter will likely encounter the same injustices and biased systems that persist today. I sincerely hope that she grows up in a society where she can exercise her rights and freedoms without facing subjugation or pressure that impedes her ability to live a fulfilling life and realize her full potential. Women still have a long way to go in the Western world, not to mention in developing countries, which is an unfortunate reality. She will face struggles as she fights against inequality and unfairness. It was this anticipated struggle that brought tears to my eyes when she was born. No one gets to choose their parents or the colour of their skin before entering this world.

We all belong to the human race, with shared needs and aspirations. Instead of causing pain to one another, our species should unite to address the challenges we face and combine our collective abilities to create a better future. Nationalism and selfish regional sentiments will not lead to substantial solutions to eradicate racism in any country in our interconnected world. In the present day, immigration to Europe has undergone significant changes compared to over 40 years ago when I embarked on my journey to Scandinavia. As a young dreamer leaving Africa back then, there were no strict visa requirements or stringent border controls. Borders were relatively open, and control measures were minimal. Moreover, people seemed to be generally friendlier towards immigrants. However, the current political climate is vastly different. Today, political parties are engaged in a competition to showcase their nationalism, often at the expense of minorities and immigrants. It has become a trend for politicians to gain votes by openly criticizing and targeting these groups. This shift in political discourse has contributed to a more challenging environment for immigrants and a less welcoming atmosphere overall.

Chapter 4

Statement for Africa

Around 40 years ago, the concept of globalization as we currently understand it had not fully taken shape. During that time, extreme poverty in Africa posed a significant obstacle for many Africans who aspired to travel abroad. Additionally, the limited contact between Africa and the rest of the world was evident, as the internet and modern telecommunication systems were not yet established. However, there was an exception in the case of The Gambia, which experienced early mass tourism primarily from Scandinavia, followed by Spain and other European countries. Despite its small size, The Gambia had a high proportion of its citizens living abroad, especially in Europe and the USA.

During the late 1980s, African countries faced mounting challenges such as increasing poverty, a severe lack of employment opportunities, and recurrent agricultural failures caused by droughts. As a result, there was a significant surge in the number of Africans, particularly Gambians, who desperately sought opportunities abroad. In response to this migration trend, Western countries implemented visa systems and other regulations specifically targeting Africans. These measures aimed to regulate and manage the flow of migrants from Africa, taking into account the economic and social impact of this movement.

As time progressed, the process of obtaining visas for Africans became increasingly challenging, with a decrease in the number of embassies and visa application centres available. Acquiring a visitor's visa, let alone a live-and-work visa became an arduous and nearly impossible task. In response to these difficulties, Africans began resorting to small boats as an alternative route to migrate to Europe, specifically targeting Grand Canaria in Spain. This led to a surge in African migrants, particularly during the 1990s, who embarked on perilous journeys lasting two weeks or even longer. Tragically, many lives were lost during these treacherous voyages. Over time, the distressing scenes of overcrowded boats and desperate African migrants, predominantly young people, became all too familiar on television screens. They risked everything in search of better opportunities in Europe, often resulting in the loss of their lives. This grim reality served as a stark reminder of the immense challenges faced by these young Africans.

However, a new migration route emerged following the downfall of Libya's former leader, Ghaddafi, which plunged the country into chaos and made it ungovernable. Many Africans, including Gambians, started embarking on treacherous journeys through the desert to reach Libya. From there, they would attempt to cross the Mediterranean Sea on flimsy boats destined for Lampedusa, Italy. Unfortunately, thousands of young lives were lost either in the unforgiving desert or at sea during these perilous journeys. The anguish experienced by their parents and loved ones was immeasurable. Despite the immense difficulties involved, this route through the desert towards Europe continues to attract numerous young Africans. It has become a significant challenge for the European Union, as governments grapple with the rise of populist anti-migration parties gaining momentum across Europe.

Halting these perilous journeys is crucial for Africans due to multiple reasons. The young lives risking everything in search of a better life represent valuable resources that the African continent desperately needs for its development. Over the past three decades, the significant "brain drain" from Africa, including my departure, has had devastating consequences for the continent. Thousands of skilled African professionals, such as teachers, nurses, doctors, and technicians, have left their home countries in pursuit of better living conditions in the West, even if it meant changing their professions or accepting jobs that were below their qualifications. This mass exodus of skilled individuals has had a profound impact on Africa's ability to build and sustain vital sectors, impeding progress and development. By choosing to stay in their home countries, these talented individuals can contribute their skills, knowledge, and expertise to the development of their communities and nations. They can play a crucial role in improving education, healthcare, technology, and other sectors that are essential for Africa's advancement.

It is vital to address the root causes that drive migration, such as poverty, unemployment, lack of opportunities, and political instability. By investing in education, creating job opportunities, fostering economic growth, and promoting good governance, African nations can create an environment where their citizens can thrive and build prosperous lives without feeling compelled to undertake dangerous journeys in search of better prospects elsewhere. Retaining skilled individuals and nurturing local talent is key to Africa's sustainable development. It is the collective responsibility of African governments, international organizations, and the global community to support initiatives that empower African youth, provide them with opportunities, and create an enabling environment for their success at home. By doing so, we can help build a brighter future for Africa and mitigate the devastating impact of the brain drain on the continent's progress.

African leaders must indeed take responsibility for addressing the issues that drive young Africans to risk their lives in search of a better future in Europe. The exodus of skilled individuals and the loss of lives in the desert are clear manifestations of abject poverty, dismal living conditions, and a sense of hopelessness. Many African leaders have failed to provide good governance, create job opportunities, and improve the overall living conditions for their people. Despite the significant role that remittances play in Africa's economy, particularly in countries like the Gambia where extreme youth unemployment rates persist, leaders have been reluctant to take decisive action to stem the outflow of talent. Remittances, which refer to the money sent back home by migrants to their country of origin, contribute significantly to the livelihoods of many African families.

To address these challenges, African leaders must prioritize tackling youth unemployment and invest in key sectors such as education, healthcare, agriculture, and infrastructure. By doing so, Africa can develop itself and reduce its reliance on development aid from the West. Strategic investments in industries and effective workforce management can help create a thriving and desirable environment for young Africans to build their lives and contribute to their communities. As Africa continues its journey towards democratic governance, there are still many obstacles to overcome. One of the most critical challenges is ensuring that the electorate is well-informed and educated to choose competent leaders capable of developing their societies. It is essential to elect leaders who prioritize good governance, strengthen institutions, and fight corruption to foster sustainable development and prosperity for all. Collectively, African leaders, civil society organizations, and the international community must work together to support initiatives that promote inclusive growth, job creation, and the empowerment of young Africans. By addressing the root causes that drive migration and providing opportunities for a better future at home, Africa can unleash its full potential and create a brighter future.

Tribal divisions do indeed play a significant role in African politics, often leading to the election of leaders based on tribal affiliations rather than their competence and ability to govern. This practice can result in the appointment of corrupt and ineffective leaders, perpetuating a cycle of corruption and incompetence within their rule. While some African countries have experienced moderate economic growth in the past decade, largely driven by trade partnerships with China and India, the continent has the potential to achieve even greater progress. However, the growth rates of certain countries, including the Gambia, which range from two to six per cent annually, are insufficient to bring about rapid development and uplift their populations from deprivation and poverty in the upcoming decade.

Amid ongoing trade conflicts between China and the West, Africa has the opportunity to emerge as a geopolitical and commercial winner in the coming decades. The continent possesses vast untapped resources, potential, and favourable demographics, positioning it to leverage its economic capabilities and forge mutually beneficial trade relationships. To realize this potential, Africa must focus on sustainable economic development, promote regional integration, address governance challenges, and nurture a favourable investment climate. By pursuing policies that prioritize inclusive growth, job creation, and poverty reduction, African nations can enable their populations to thrive and improve their quality of life.

African leaders must prioritize the interests of their people above tribal affiliations and work towards building strong, transparent, and accountable governance systems. This requires promoting meritocracy, fostering unity and social cohesion, and combating corruption and nepotism. Furthermore, regional cooperation and integration can enhance Africa's competitiveness in the global market. By strengthening intra-African trade, harmonizing regulations, and investing in infrastructure that connects countries, Africa can create a larger market, attract more investment, and accelerate economic growth.

African nations should also prioritize investment in education, healthcare, and technology, as well as diversify their economies beyond resource extraction. By developing industries, fostering innovation, and promoting entrepreneurship, Africa can reduce its vulnerability to commodity price fluctuations and build a more resilient and sustainable economy. In conclusion, by addressing governance challenges, promoting regional integration, and pursuing inclusive and sustainable economic development, Africa can unlock its full potential and achieve significant progress in the years ahead.

African leaders need to prioritize the long-term interests of their nations and work towards a prosperous and united continent.

Indeed, African nations that embrace democracy, strengthen institutions and make wise investments are more likely to experience accelerated development compared to those following alternative paths. While the middle class is expanding in Africa and certain countries have made notable progress over the past decade, the continent still faces a tarnished reputation in the Western world, often perceived as relatively backward. This perception has hindered significant direct foreign investment, as investors heavily rely on mainstream media for information. Unfortunately, the media in the West often displays little interest in highlighting positive and noteworthy developments from the continent. As a result, many investors and the general population in the West still hold outdated perceptions of Africa, reminiscent of the challenges faced in the 1980s, such as widespread famine, conflict, and disorder. This perception may not accurately reflect the current reality and the progress Africa has made in various aspects.

To gain a broader perspective and challenge these outdated perceptions, it is worth exploring resources like Professor Hans Rosling's book "Factfulness: Ten Reasons We're Wrong About the World—and Why Things Are Better Than You Think." Such resources provide valuable insights into Africa's growth and ongoing development. The unity of African nations in establishing a free trade zone, speaking with a unified voice and even considering currency unions represent the continent's means of self-empowerment and advancement. By fostering collaboration, African countries can strengthen their collective bargaining power, attract more investment, and improve economic integration within the continent. This unity is crucial for Africa to assert itself on the global stage and reshape its narrative, showcasing its potential and the positive transformations taking place across the continent.

African nations must indeed continue their efforts in promoting democratic governance, strengthening institutions, and making strategic investments to drive growth and infrastructural development. These steps are crucial in challenging outdated perceptions, attracting investment, and propelling the continent towards greater progress and prosperity. One practical step that has been overdue in Africa is knowledge-sharing among nations. Leaders need to recognize the wealth of knowledge and resources that the diaspora can bring back to the continent, contributing to its rapid growth.

However, the business environment in Africa still faces significant challenges, including widespread corruption and an inefficient bureaucracy that hampers progress. Remarkably, there are Africans who hold influential positions and possess experiences in multinational corporations, international institutions, and various establishments. Unfortunately, these individuals are often not fully welcome to serve in African governments and institutions. Regrettably, many African leaders tend to overlook the tremendous potential of engaging the diaspora in their countries of origin. Obstacles, whether rooted in legislation or outright rejection, hinder the effective involvement of the diaspora. Nevertheless, there is encouraging news: a considerable number of Africans in the West are willing and prepared to return and contribute, armed with qualifications, experience, and education.

To fully harness the potential of the diaspora, African leaders must create an enabling environment that encourages their active participation. This includes reforming legislation, streamlining bureaucratic processes, and establishing mechanisms for diaspora engagement. By leveraging the expertise and resources of the diaspora, African nations can benefit from their contributions and accelerate progress across various sectors. Furthermore, African governments should work towards creating a more favourable business environment that tackles corruption, enhances transparency, and streamlines procedures.

By addressing these challenges, African nations can attract both diaspora and foreign investment, stimulate economic growth, and create opportunities for sustainable development. African leaders need to recognize the immense value of the diaspora and actively involve them in the development processes of their countries. By fostering collaboration and leveraging the diaspora's skills, knowledge, and networks, Africa can tap into its full potential and achieve greater prosperity for its people.

However, African governments are yet unprepared to fully embrace and integrate this well-prepared diaspora, despite their qualifications. The inclusion of this group has the potential to rapidly transform Africa into a progressive continent, effectively addressing numerous challenges.

With their ability to efficiently manage institutions, enhance work morale, combat corruption, and achieve set objectives, this group possesses the capacity and transferable skills needed to drive accelerated development. They represent a valuable resource that would serve the continent's best interests.

African leaders would be remiss to ignore the immense value and talent that the diaspora brings, as it holds the key to significant advancements for the continent.

Embracing and leveraging the skills of this diaspora would yield remarkable achievements for Africa. Failing to recognize this would be a missed opportunity of great consequence for the continent.

Milton Keynes UK
Ingram Content Group UK Ltd.
UKHW022119100124
435829UK00004B/61